NAVIGATION HANDBOOK

MELANIE BARTLETT FRIN

© RYA/Melanie Bartlett
First published 2003
This edition published 2013
Reprinted October 2014, October 2015,
September 2016, August 2017,
September 2018, November 2019

The Royal Yachting Association
RYA House, Ensign Way,
Hamble, Southampton,
Hampshire SO31 4YA
Tel: 02380 604100
Web: www.rya.org.uk

Follow us on Twitter @RYAPublications
or on YouTube

We welcome feedback on our
publications at publications@rya.org.uk

You can check content updates for RYA
publications at www.rya.org.uk/go/bookschangelog

ISBN 978-1-906435943
RYA Order Code G6

Cover design: Pete Galvin
Typesetting and design: Velveo Design
Proofreading and indexing: Alan Thatcher
Printed in China through World Print Ltd.

Sustainable
Forests

EMAS
VERIFIED
ENVIRONMENTAL
MANAGEMENT

ACKNOWLEDGEMENTS

Patrick Roach, Christel Clear, Dalgleish Images, Chris Tibbs, Dan Nicholson, UKHO, Plastimo, Garmin, ICS, Imray Norie Laurie & Wilson, Nautical Data Ltd, RNLI, Velveo Design, Melanie Bartlett.

FOREWORD

Navigation is one of the most fundamental skills required for a safe and enjoyable time on the water. To the newcomer, the jargon, strange instruments and wide variety of navigational techniques may at first seem daunting. Whilst the fundamentals of navigation have remained unchanged for centuries, the continuous development of new technology means that we have more tools than ever before to help us find our way.

This book is designed to provide the reader with a sound understanding of the basic principles of navigation as well as providing insight into the ways in which electronic navigation can be used to best effect. The combination of both traditional and electronic navigational techniques will ensure the development of a 'well rounded' and competent navigator.

Melanie Bartlett is an RYA Yachtmaster Instructor, journalist and author with a wealth of knowledge across a wide variety of marine-related subjects. Her lifetime of experience in practical navigation along with her clear and effective style of communicating the subject will provide you with the perfect platform from which to develop your own navigational skills.

Richard Falk MRIN
RYA Director of Training & Qualifications

CONTENTS

INTRODUCING NAVIGATION

Navigation can be defined as the process of planning and carrying out the movement of transport of all kinds from one place to another, or as controlling or directing travel.

Basic Principles of Navigation

It doesn't have to be a terribly clever or high-tech process. Some of the most primitive animals on the planet navigate by setting off towards something that attracts them – such as a source of food or warmth – or away from something that repels them. If they bump into something on the way, they respond simply by changing direction and trying again until they find their way round the obstruction.

Humans start off in much the same way! By the time we have learned to walk, however, we have all started to develop much more sophisticated navigational techniques. Even a toddler is quite capable of finding her way around her home. She can get from one room to another and avoid some of the hazards on the way.

By the time the toddler has grown to be a teenager, she is almost certainly quite an accomplished navigator. Even if she thinks she has no sense of direction, she could probably find her way around an unfamiliar town by following signposts or directions, and may well be able to use a simple map to create her own set of directions without having to ask anyone else.

By visualising the map as a diagrammatic bird's eye view of the shopping mall, and herself as an ant-sized creature walking around on it, it's also easy enough for her to pick out a route from her starting point (between the shops coloured blue in the bottom left-hand corner of the map) to her destination (the sports shop, also coloured blue, near the top right-hand corner). She could, for instance, set off past the pet shop, turn right at the garden, and turn left at the café, expecting to find the sports shop on the right-hand side, about halfway between the café and the supermarket.

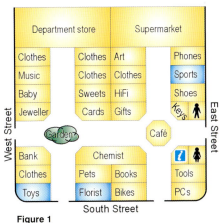

Figure 1

Alternatively, she could go back out of the shopping mall, turn left past the florist and bike shop, turn left again into East Street, and go back into the mall between the toilets. This time, she needs to turn right at the café instead of left, and walk past the key-cutter and shoe shop to the sports shop.

As adults, what may be quite an adventure for a thirteen-year-old has become so commonplace that for most of the time we work out where we are and how we are progressing almost without thinking about it.

Navigating at sea seems very different. The principles, though, are surprisingly similar.

Suppose, for instance, that we are in Port Rampton, at Quarry Marina (represented by the

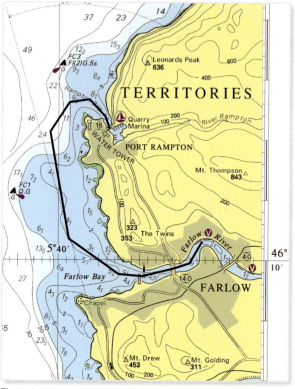

Figure 2

magenta 'boat' symbol in the chart extract in Figure 2) and want to go to the visitors' pontoons in the Farlow River (represented by the circular "V" symbols).

The marine chart, just like the map of the shopping mall, is a diagrammatic representation of the area, from which it's easy to see that once we have gone under the bridge out of the marina we shall need to head out of Rampton Bay before turning left around the headland. Keeping roughly parallel to the coastline, we'll go past the town of Port Rampton, heading towards another headland with a chapel on its tip, until we can turn left into the Farlow River. We'll go under another bridge before finding the visitors' pontoons on the left-hand side, at the apex of a right-hand bend.

Like the teenager in the shopping mall, we need to know where we are starting from and where we're hoping to get to, and plan a route between the two.

There are three big differences between marine navigation and land navigation on roads or in shopping centres:

- At sea we can head in almost any direction without the constraints of kerbs or walls.
- The sea itself is moving, so we don't necessarily move in the direction the boat is pointing.
- Hazards, such as rocks and sandbanks, are often hidden below the surface.

2 | POSITION

Position is one of the fundamentals of navigation. You usually need to know where you are, you almost always need to know where you are trying to get to, and you definitely need to know where the hazards are that you are trying to avoid.

This doesn't mean that your knowledge of position has to be particularly precise, or that it has to be expressed in technical-sounding language. To say that the Seven Stones Light vessel is 'fourteen miles west of Land's End', for instance, probably means a lot more to most people than to say it is at 50° 03'.58N 006° 04'.28W. It is also a lot easier to remember, and less susceptible to human errors – such as writing 50° 05'.38N instead of 50° 03'.58N.

On the other hand it is very useful to have a method of specifying a position anywhere on Earth that is unambiguous and can be understood by navigators of all nationalities, without any local knowledge whatsoever, yet can be as precise as we want it to be – to a matter of millimetres, if necessary. Latitude and longitude enable us to do just that.

Latitude and Longitude

Our world is a ball of rock, just less than 13,000 kilometres in diameter, spinning through space. It is not a perfect sphere: apart from surface irregularities, such as hills, valleys, and seas, it is also slightly squashed. This distortion is only about a third of 1 per cent, so for many practical purposes it can be ignored, and we can visualise the Earth as though it were a perfect sphere whose surface is covered by an invisible network of lines, rather like the grid that is used to help find particular towns or villages in a road atlas (Figure 3).

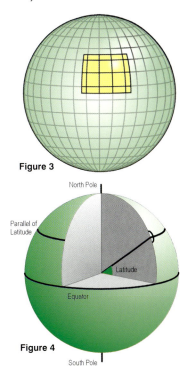

Figure 3

Figure 4

Unlike the grid on a street map or road atlas, however, the graticule of latitude and longitude is not entirely arbitrary, but is based on a few natural reference points.

The most important of these natural references are the north and south Poles (Figure 4). They represent the ends of the Earth's axis of spin. Exactly midway between the poles, at right angles to them, and running around the fattest part of the Earth, is the Equator.

Latitude

The formal definition of latitude is 'the angle which the perpendicular to the Earth's surface at a place makes with the plane of the Equator'. That can be difficult to visualise, so a useful working definition is:

Latitude is distance from the Equator, expressed as an angle, measured in degrees at the centre of the Earth.

Latitude by itself is no good at defining a particular position. Falmouth, for instance, is 50 degrees north of the Equator. So are Frankfurt, Prague, and Winnipeg, to name but three. If you were to join together all the places that share the same latitude, the result would be a line running round the world. It's parallel to the Equator, so it's called a parallel of latitude.

On most maps and charts, parallels appear as horizontal lines, running from side to side.

Longitude

The corresponding vertical lines are called meridians. They run from pole to pole, dividing the world into segments as though it were a giant orange (Figure 5).

The Equator was a pretty obvious reference from which to measure latitude. Unfortunately, none of the countless meridians which could be drawn from pole to pole stood out as an obvious candidate to be the prime meridian from which to measure longitude. Until the latter part of the 19th century, this meant that different countries adopted different prime meridians – usually based on their own capital cities. In 1884, however, an international conference agreed a world standard, taking one of the telescopes at Britain's Greenwich Observatory as its reference point.

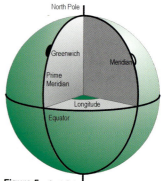

Figure 5

The formal definition of longitude is 'the angle between the plane of the Prime Meridian and the meridian of the place'.

Combining latitude and longitude enables us to specify particular positions. Frankfurt, for instance, is at 50°N 009°E, while Falmouth is at 50°N 005°W. Bear in mind, though, that the Earth is so big that 1 degree of latitude at its surface is over a hundred kilometres. To specify positions more accurately, each degree can be subdivided into sixtieths, called minutes. Each minute can be further subdivided, either into sixtieths called seconds or, more commonly, into tenths, hundredths, or thousandths.

The position of a buoy, for instance, may be given as 50° 04'.92N 005° 04'.88W. Notice that latitude is given first, followed by longitude, and that their directions (north or south and east or west) are always included.

Horizontal Datums

Over the years and across the continents and oceans numerous mapmakers and mathematicians have come up with their own ways of defining the shape of the Earth, while seamen, navigators and surveyors have worked out their positions using whatever references were available, such as the visible horizon. The trouble is that because the Earth is not really a perfect sphere, spinning about a fixed axis, and because it is very difficult to measure 'vertical' accurately, they were using several different 'centres' on which to base their measurements of latitude and longitude.

This means that history has given us many different graticules of latitude and longitude – known as horizontal datums – which don't quite marry up with each other. Until recently, for instance, charts of British waters were drawn using a horizontal datum known as Ordnance Survey Great Britain 1936 (OSGB 36), while charts of the rest of Northern Europe were based on one called the European Datum 1950 (ED 50). ED 50 is based on the assumption that the Earth is slightly bigger and slightly more squashed than the British model.

The result is that the latitude and longitude of a fixed object vary, depending on the horizontal datum to which they are referred.

Until relatively recently this was of little practical significance to navigators. The advent of space travel, intercontinental missiles and satellite navigation systems, however, brought with it the need for a worldwide standard. Fortunately, they also provided the means of achieving it.

The worldwide standard that is now most widely used for marine charts is known as the World Geodetic System 1984 (WGS 84). It's not the only one: a few charts were based on its predecessor (WGS 72), and many new charts of European waters are drawn on a later datum called the European Terrestrial Reference System 1989 (ETRS 89). There are technical differences between WGS 84 and ETRS 89, arising from the fact that Europe and America are drifting apart (at the rate of a few centimetres per year).

For practical navigational purposes, the discrepancies between ETRS 89 and WGS 84 are negligible. As Figure 6 shows, however, the discrepancies between WGS 84/ETRS 89, ED 50, and OSGB 36 are quite enough to be significant.

Round Island lighthouse, for instance, is at 49° 58'.702N 6° 19'.335W, according to the OSGB 36 datum, but is at 49° 58'.797N 6° 19'.294W according to ED 50 – an apparent discrepancy of nearly 200 metres!

In some parts of the world, particularly parts of the Pacific Ocean, datum discrepancies can amount to 2 kilometres or more.

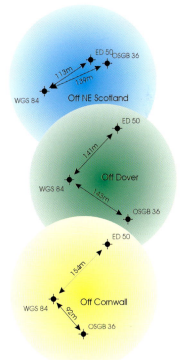

Figure 6

Dealing with Datums

If you are navigating only by traditional methods, in which latitude and longitude are almost irrelevant, even these large datum discrepancies can usually be ignored altogether, just as they were in years gone by.

However, if you are using any kind of electronic 'navigator', such as a satellite navigation system or an electronic chart plotter, it is important to make sure that your positioning system and your chart are referring to the same datum.

On British Admiralty charts, the datum on which the chart is based is always stated in the information panel just below the title. You can't change the datum of the chart, so you have to change the datum of your positioning system. There are usually two (sometimes three) options:

- Automatic.
- Arithmetic.
- Manual.

Dealing with Datums – Automatic Conversion

GPS satellite navigation receivers invariably use WGS 84 as their 'default' datum. All but a tiny minority, however, can be set up to carry out an automatic conversion into any of several dozen (sometimes several hundred) alternative datums. The procedure for doing so varies from one model to another, so it is essential to check with the instruction manual to find out how to do it, and to make sure that the navigator is switched to the appropriate datum for the chart you are using at the time.

Suppose, for instance, you are planning a passage from the south coast of England to the Channel Islands. As part of the planning process, you are likely to want to store important positions such as harbour entrances in the navigator's memory. These stored positions are known as waypoints, and are covered in more detail on page 69. Your detailed charts of the south coast may well be drawn to the OSGB 36 datum, while your Channel Island charts are drawn on ED 50. This means that while you are dealing with the charts of the English coast, you should keep the GPS set up to display OSGB 36. When you turn your attention to the charts of the Channel Islands, however, you should also turn the GPS to ED 50.

If, at this stage, you refer back to an English waypoint that you stored as 50° 36'.57N 2° 26.49W, you may well find that it appears as 50° 36'.656N 2° 26'.486W. That is because the GPS set has converted it.

When you come to make the real passage, you again need to check that the GPS is set to the correct datum (OSGB 36) when you are leaving the English coast, and switch it over to the ED 50 datum somewhere in mid-Channel.

Dealing with Datums – Arithmetic Conversion

Charts drawn to any datum other than WGS 84 or ETRS 89 include a note explaining how to convert positions shown by a GPS set operating on its default datum (WGS 84) to the appropriate datum for the chart. It may, for instance, say:

SATELLITE-DERIVED POSITIONS
Positions obtained from satellite navigation systems are frequently referred to WGS Datum; such positions should be moved 0.06 minutes NORTHWARD and 0.08 minutes EASTWARD to agree with this chart.

Converting a position shown by a GPS set to one that can be plotted (marked) on the chart is a simple matter of following the instructions. Suppose the GPS display reads 50°49'.372N 1°16'.157E:

50° 49'.372N	1° 16'.157E
+ 0'.060N	+ 0'.080E
50° 49'.432N	1° 16'.237E

The position should be plotted as 50° 49'.432N 1° 16'.237E.

In this particular case, the conversions had the same names (north and east) as the latitude and longitude. If the names are opposite – an easterly conversion being applied to a westerly longitude, for instance, the conversion has to be subtracted. Suppose the GPS display had read 49° 50'.372N 1° 16'.157W:

49° 50'.372N	1° 16'.157W
+ 0'.060N	- 0'.080E
49° 50'.432N	1° 16'.077W

The position should be plotted as 49° 50'.432N 1° 16'.077W.

Care is also called for when waypoints taken from an ED 50 or OSGB 36 chart are being applied to a GPS set that is referring to WGS 84 positions. Remember that the instructions on the chart show how to convert WGS positions to suit the chart, not vice versa. This means that to convert charted waypoints to WGS, the conversion instructions have to be reversed. For a waypoint at 49° 26'.340N 2° 21'.050W, for instance, the conversion would go like this:

49° 26'.340N	2° 21'.050W
- 0'.060S	+ 0'.080W
49° 26'.280N	2° 21'.130W

The fact that the conversions are only given to two decimal places makes them look somewhat imprecise compared with the three decimal places that are usually shown by a satellite navigator. Nevertheless, they have the advantage of having been calculated using significantly more sophisticated algorithms than those used by most civilian GPS receivers. The big snag with this arithmetical method is that it is tedious and very susceptible to human error. In general, it is better to rely on the automatic method.

Dealing with Datums – Manual Conversion

Some GPS sets also offer a position-offset or user-defined datum facility. In effect, this allows the user to give the GPS receiver the appropriate conversion data for a particular chart. The computer that is built into the GPS receiver will then take care of all the arithmetic.

This facility is useful if you are dealing with a chart whose horizontal datum is not specified or if it is one that is not recognised by your particular GPS. In such circumstances, it's easy enough to find the appropriate conversion figures by comparing the actual position of some fixed landmark (such as a harbour wall) with its charted position.

Generally, though, position offsets and user-defined datums should be used only as a last resort; it is too easy to apply them in the wrong direction or to continue applying them when they should have been switched off.

Dealing with Datums – the Future

The problems posed by the use of different horizontal datums are gradually disappearing. Already, many charts have been redrawn to WGS 84 or to almost identical datums such as ETRS 89. Even now, though, charts of some of the remoter parts of the world are still based on surveys that were carried out in the 18th century, using sextants and lead lines. It is likely to be many years before these charts are converted and republished.

Summary
- Parallels and meridians form a worldwide grid system.
  - Parallels of latitude are invisible lines, parallel to the Equator.
  - Meridians are invisible lines from pole to pole, at right angles to the parallels.
- Position at sea can be expressed in terms of latitude and longitude.
  - The latitude of a place is its distance north or south of the Equator.
  - The longitude of a place is its distance east or west of the prime (Greenwich) meridian.
  - Latitude and longitude are both expressed as angles.
- The Earth is not a perfect sphere, so it has many possible 'centres', and many possible grids of latitude and longitude that do not quite match up with each other.

3 | DIRECTION

Direction is another of the fundamentals of navigation. It is so important that navigators seldom refer simply to 'direction' as such, but use a variety of technical terms such as course, heading, bearing, and track to refer to specific types of direction – such as the direction from one object to another, or the direction a boat is pointing.

Even so, we don't always need to express direction in particularly precise terms or in technical-sounding language. To say "the southbound tide starts a couple of hours before Low Water", for instance, may be a useful and accurate generalisation. The more technical-sounding "the tide starts flowing 180° at Low Water -2", on the other hand, would be wrong, because it implies a level of accuracy far greater than it actually achieves.

The formal definitions of north, south, east and west are all based on the Earth's rotation:

- East is the direction in which the Earth rotates.
- West is the opposite direction to east.
- North is the direction from a point on the Earth's surface towards the pole that would be on the left-hand side of an observer facing east.
- South is the opposite of north.

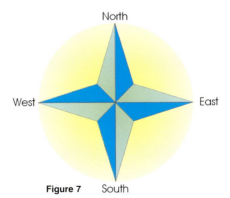

Figure 7

As most of us would have to think very long and hard to work out which way the Earth spins, these definitions are of purely academic interest. It is far more useful simply to remember the diagram (Figure 7) or to visualise a simple compass card.

Different Kinds of Direction

As navigators, we have to deal with many different kinds of direction. To distinguish between them each one has a different name. Each of these technical terms has its own, specific meaning: course and heading for instance, are not interchangeable!

Bearing is the direction of one object from another.

Course is the direction the vessel is intended to be steered.

Heading is the direction in which the vessel is actually pointing at any given moment. It is very seldom exactly the same as the course.

Track Angle is the direction the vessel is actually moving over the surface of the Earth. The effects of wind and tide mean that it is not usually the same as the heading. In practice, the word 'angle' is often omitted. Ground Track, Course Made Good (CMG) and Course over Ground (CoG) all mean the same thing.

Water Track is used by marine navigators to refer to the direction the vessel is moving through the water. It is sometimes called Wake Course.

Directions between these four cardinal points can be given names, too (Figure 8). South-east, for instance, is midway between south and east, south-west is midway between south and west, and so on. Further sub-division produces eight quarter cardinal points, such as south-south-west, west-south-west. Even these can be sub-divided to produce 16 by-points, with names such as north by west – meaning 'a little bit west of north'.

Directions could be specified to a precision of just over five degrees by a further subdivision into half points.

Figure 8

It's very difficult to steer a small boat any more accurately than this, so the points system survived in yachts and small commercial craft until the latter half of the 20th century. Cardinal points, half cardinals and quarter cardinals are still used for approximate directions (in weather forecasts, for instance) but for navigational purposes they have been almost entirely replaced by the three-figure notation.

Three-figure notation is now virtually universal. Directions are referred to as angles, measured in degrees, counting clockwise from north, so east is 090°, southeast is 135° and so on (Figure 9).

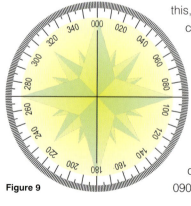

Figure 9

Directions should always be written and spoken as three distinct figures. This isn't pure pedantry! Many small boat compasses are marked at 10-degree intervals, with the final zeros left off to save space, so if you ask a helmsman to steer "35" there is a very real risk that he will steer 350° (to the 35 mark) rather than the 035° you intended.

Measuring Direction – in the Real World

In order to measure direction, any boat should carry at least one compass. Most carry two or more. One is usually fixed to the boat itself and is used to show the direction she is pointing, so it is called the steering compass. The other is a smaller, hand-held version used for measuring bearings, and is known as a hand-bearing compass.

Sometimes one compass can be used to do both jobs: a hand-bearing compass mounted in a suitable bracket, for instance, can be used as a steering compass, and is particularly suitable for cruising dinghies, small keelboats and RIBs. At the other extreme, many ships use a sighting arrangement called a pelorus or azimuth circle mounted on top of the main compass for taking bearings.

It's not unusual, though, for even quite small yachts to have several compasses. A yacht with tiller steering, for instance, may well have one steering compass on each side of the cockpit; a flybridge motor cruiser usually has one at each steering position. There may also be one at the chart table or over the skipper's berth, and another to control an autopilot.

Magnetic Compasses

Although there are several alternatives available, the overwhelming majority of yachts and small motor boats use compasses that work by sensing the direction of the Earth's magnetic field. Essentially, the Earth behaves as though there is a gigantic bar magnet embedded in its core. Of course, there isn't really a magnet there, and it is still a matter of some conjecture exactly what is going on to produce the effect. Nevertheless, for centuries, navigators have been able to make use of the fact that a free-swinging, needle-shaped magnet will turn to point north-south.

Small compasses, such as the ones used for backpacking and orienteering on land, still use a single magnetised needle as a north pointer. Most marine compasses, however, use several magnets, or a single ring-shaped magnet mounted on a circular card. The card is marked with a scale of degrees or compass points, and is suspended in a bowl filled with a mixture of water and alcohol. Of course, there are many variations on this theme: some compasses are designed to be looked at from above; some are designed to be seen edgeways on, and there are even some that are intended to be viewed from underneath. The extent of the damping also varies: compasses intended for motor boats in particular are usually much more heavily-damped than those aimed at sailing boats in order to cope with the rapid pitching motion.

An alternative kind of magnetic compass, known as a flux gate, has no moving parts, but uses electronics to sense the direction of the Earth's magnetic field. This has enormous advantages: a flux gate compass is compact, can easily be linked to other electronic equipment such as an autopilot or radar, and its output can be automatically processed to correct for errors. Because the sensor and display can be separate it's even possible to reduce errors at source by mounting the sensor wherever it will be least affected by stray magnetic fields. Apart from its dependence on electrical power, the big weakness of a flux gate compass is that it is very susceptible to tilt. For every degree that the sensor is tilted, it can easily produce 2 degrees of direction error. This problem can be overcome electronically, but most flux gate compasses also have quite sophisticated stabilising arrangements.

How a Flux Gate Works

Like transformers, electric motors and petrol engine ignition systems, a flux gate compass depends on the intimate relationship between electricity and magnetism, and in particular on the fact that if you pass an electric current through a coil of wire that has been wound around a suitable metal core, the core will become a magnet. Which end is the south pole and which is the north pole depends on the direction of the current flow, so if you pass an alternating current through the coil, the poles change ends every time the current reverses.

If you wrap another coil around this electromagnet, the opposite happens: every time the polarity of the magnet changes it generates an electrical current in the outer coil.

In a flux gate there are two cores, side by side. Their inner (primary) coils are both made from a single length of wire, wound in one direction around one, but in the opposite direction round the other. The result is that when an alternating 'exciter' current is applied to them, they form a pair of perfectly matched magnets, pointing in opposite directions, and therefore cancelling each other out. In a magnetically 'clean' environment, this would mean that no current is ever generated in the outer (secondary) coil. When the cores are lined up with the Earth's magnetic field, however, this delicate balance is upset, producing pulses of electricity in the secondary winding. These pulses are most pronounced when the core is pointing north-south, and disappear altogether when it points east-west.

Practical flux gate compasses use several flux gates arranged in a circle, and work by comparing the voltage created in the output windings of each one.

Compass Errors

Variation

All magnetic compasses – needle, swinging card or flux gate – depend on the assumption that the Earth's magnetic field is lined up with its north-south axis. Unfortunately that isn't quite true: in 2003, the Earth's magnetic North Pole was nearly 900 kilometres away from the real North Pole.

This means that there is a discrepancy between the north shown by a magnetic compass and the north represented by the meridians on a map or chart. The discrepancy is called

Where is the North Pole?

The magnetic North Pole is constantly moving. Every day it traces out an oval path about 85 kilometres long. The centre of that oval path also moves. Its speed and direction vary but over the past century it has averaged about 40 kilometres per year.

When it was first located, in 1831, it was at 70°N 97°W on the north coast of Canada.

In 2003, it was at 72°N 112°W.

If it continues at its present rate, it could pass about 200km from the True North Pole in 2020, and reach Siberia by about 2050.

variation[1] because it varies from year to year (as the magnetic North Pole moves) and from place to place.

At the moment (2013) variation in parts of New Zealand is about 25°W, while in parts of Alaska and NW Canada it is over 20°E, but in southern Norway and the Netherlands it is zero. Around the UK it is greatest on the west coast of Ireland (6°W) and gradually reducing.

The amount of variation can always be found by looking on the navigational charts, where it can usually be found in each compass rose (see page 14) or else in the information panel just below the chart title.

It will be given in the form 5° 15'W 2000 (9'E). This means that magnetic North was 5° 15' west of True North in 2000, and was moving eastwards by 9 minutes per year (9'E). In 2003, therefore, it will have changed by 3 x 9' = 27'.

As the variation was originally west, and the change is eastward, the variation must be reducing, so it has become 5° 15'W - 27' = 4° 48'W (Note that there are 60 minutes in a degree). For practical navigation purposes, though, this level of accuracy is unnecessary, and the answer can be rounded off to 5°W.

What this means is that if you measure the bearing of a lighthouse as 130° using a hand-bearing compass, the True bearing of the lighthouse is 125°. If you then look at the chart and find that you need to steer 240° (True), it means that the helmsman, using a magnetic compass, needs to steer 245°.

Once you know about an error, you're usually at least half way to correcting it, and in this case it is a matter of simple arithmetic:

To convert from Magnetic to True add easterly variation or subtract westerly variation.

To convert from True to Magnetic add westerly variation or subtract easterly variation.

There are several mnemonics to help remember this. One is the simple rhyme, Error west, Compass Best; Error east, Compass Least (best in this case meaning biggest!). Another is the 'CadET rule', which is a reminder that to get from C (Compass) to T (True) you have to 'ad' (add) E (Easterly errors).

---

[1] Variation is often referred to as 'Magnetic Declination', particularly by geographers and scientists. For navigational purposes, variation is the more common term, and is better because it cannot be confused with declination, which refers to a completely different factor in astro-navigation.

Magnetic Anomalies

The Earth's magnetic field is very weak, so it is easily distorted by large metal structures such as wrecks, pipelines, and jetties. Fortunately, these man-made structures are generally relatively small, so their effects on a compass are extremely localised. Various types of naturally occurring magnetic material can have a more pronounced effect, and cover a wider area.

Where such magnetic anomalies are known to occur, they are marked on the relevant navigational chart. There is very little you can do about magnetic anomalies, other than to be aware of their existence and to bear in mind that, if you are in an affected area, the compass will be less reliable than usual. It will not, however, spin on its axis or self-destruct!

Deviation

Significant magnetic anomalies are relatively rare, and their effects are generally short-lived. Almost every boat, however, includes a number of magnetic components, including a few such as electric motors and loudspeakers that include powerful magnets, and others, such as electric wiring, that sometimes generate magnetic fields. The boat, in other words, carries its own magnetic anomalies around with it. The individual components may be small compared with an undersea deposit of iron ore but they are very much closer to the compass, so they are responsible for a third type of compass error, known as deviation.

Deviation is almost always present to some extent, but it changes as the boat alters course and, to a lesser degree, as she heels or pitches. It is easy to see why, if you think of a boat with a magnetic object such as a radio mounted just ahead of the steering compass.

When the boat is heading north (Figure 10), the north-seeking pole of the compass needle is attracted towards the object. Of course, this doesn't matter because that is the direction the needle should be pointing anyway. Much the same applies when the boat is heading south.

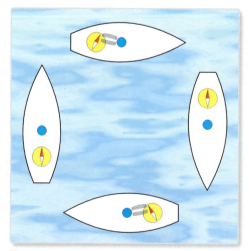

Figure 10

When the boat is heading east or west, however, you can visualise the compass needle being pulled in two directions at once, with the Earth's magnetic field trying to keep it in north-south alignment while the magnetic object on board tries to turn it east-west. If the deviating object were to one side of the compass – a steel gas bottle in a cockpit locker, for instance – the principle would be the same, but its effect would be different: deviation would be negligible when the boat is heading east or west, and at its maximum when she is heading north or south.

Things that are directly underneath (or above) the compass have virtually no effect so long as the boat is upright. As she heels over, though, the geometry changes. An object that was originally below the compass moves to port when the boat heels to starboard, and vice versa. As soon as it is on one side of the compass rather than directly below, it starts to have a deviating effect, producing what is known as 'heeling error'.

In real-life, most compasses are surrounded by many deviating influences, each of which has its own particular characteristics. Their combined effect, however, can be measured. A skilled compass adjuster can even counteract their influence, to reduce deviation, by fitting small magnets and iron rods in and around the compass bowl. Some compasses even have corrector magnets built in, adjusted by screws on the outside of the bowl.

Compass adjustment is a skilled and specialised job, but every navigator needs to know how to keep deviation to a minimum, how to check it, and what to do about it.

Minimising Deviation

As deviation is caused by magnetic objects near the compass, the obvious preventative measure is to keep magnets and magnetic materials as far away from the compass as possible. In the case of an electronic instrument designed specifically for marine use, look for a label indicating its 'compass safe distance' – the distance at which it will deflect a compass by less than one degree.

Be particularly wary of movable objects such as toolboxes, tinned food, portable radios, and mobile phones.

Checking for Deviation

There are many different ways of checking and measuring deviation. Essentially, they all involve comparing the direction indicated by the compass with some known direction – a process known as swinging the compass. A compass adjuster will carry out a swing before and after making any adjustment, but it's a good idea to do it yourself at least once a year, and certainly after any repair or maintenance work that might have affected it.

The most straightforward method is known as a 'swing by distant objects'. It involves taking the boat to an accurately known position and then turning it round to point at each of several distant landmarks in turn. The true bearing of each landmark can be found from the navigational chart and converted to a magnetic bearing (see page 17). The difference between the magnetic bearing and the bearing shown by the boat's compass represents the deviation on that particular heading.

Suppose, for instance, that the chart shows that the True bearing from our present position to Berry Head lighthouse is 172°, but when the boat is pointing straight at the lighthouse, the steering compass reads 174°. Variation is 6° west.

First, convert the charted bearing from True to Magnetic using the CadET rule (see page 17):

> 172° (True)
> + 6° W
> ───────────
> 178° (Magnetic)

Then, find the difference between the Magnetic and Compass bearings:

> 178° (Magnetic)
> - 174° (Compass)
> ───────────
> 4°

Finally, name the deviation east or west, according to the 'Error east, Compass Least' rule (see page 17). In this particular example, the compass bearing is 4° less than the magnetic bearing, so the deviation is 4°E.

Exactly how accurate your initial position needs to be depends on the accuracy you hope to achieve and the distance to your distant objects. An accuracy of 1 degree can be achieved if you know your position to within 100 metres and use landmarks that are 3 miles away. If the landmarks are 6 miles away, the position accuracy can be correspondingly less – 200m. This level of accuracy can easily be achieved by motoring in slow circles around a charted wooden post or beacon, by finding the intersection of two transits (see page 80), or by GPS.

A single transit (two objects that appear to be in line with each other) is useful for a quick check of the compass, because it is easy to draw a line on the chart passing through both objects that represents your line of sight. When the two objects appear to be in line with each other, you must be somewhere on that line. If, at the same moment, you point the boat straight at the two objects, then its heading, as shown by the steering compass, should correspond with the magnetic bearing of the transit (Figure 11).

Be careful, though, as in tidal waters or if there is a cross wind there may be a distinct difference between the heading required to point straight at the transit (for a compass check) and the heading required to stay on the transit line (see page 80).

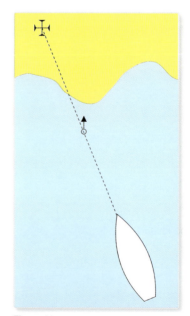

Figure 11

CDR. **R. Rackstraw** RN

Compass Adjuster and Marine Surveyor
Dartmouth (01803) 732338

Proud Maiden

25 May 2003

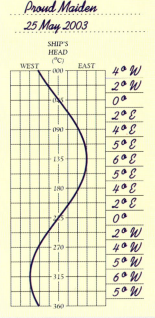

Figure 12

Correcting for Deviation

Once a compass adjuster has done his best to remove deviation, he will draw up a deviation card, showing any residual errors that could not be removed.

If the compass has not been professionally adjusted, it is even more important to produce your own deviation card (Figure 12) summarising the deviation and showing how it changes.

If the deviation is very small – less than about two or three degrees – it is common practice to ignore it, on the basis that it is impossible to steer that accurately anyway. On the other hand, correcting for small amounts of deviation is a very simple arithmetical process, identical to the procedure for correcting for variation:

To convert from Compass to Magnetic add easterly deviation or subtract westerly deviation.

To convert from Magnetic to Compass add westerly deviation or subtract easterly deviation.

The mnemonics that are used to handle variation are equally applicable to deviation (see page 17).

Deviation and Hand-Bearing Compasses

The information given on the deviation card is only true if the magnetic geometry of the boat is unchanged. If you move a gas bottle from one side of the cockpit to another, it could have an effect.

The effect would be even more noticeable if you moved the compass, because you would almost certainly be taking it away from some deviating influences but towards others that could well be pulling the needle in a completely different direction.

This means that it is impossible to produce a deviation card for a hand-bearing compass which, by its very nature, may be used anywhere on the boat. Rather than risk applying a 'correction' for deviation, which could make matters worse, it is normal practice to assume that the deviation of a hand-bearing compass is zero.

Bear in mind, though, that this does not mean that a hand-bearing compass is immune from deviation. If it were possible to produce a deviation-free magnetic compass, then that technology would certainly have been applied to steering compasses.

It is a good idea to get into the habit of using a hand-bearing compass only in areas that are well clear of obvious sources of deviation. Never be seduced by the suggestion that a hand-bearing compass can be used to check the deviation of a steering compass.

The error of a hand-bearing compass can change significantly even in the space of a few metres, but it's possible to carry out a simple snapshot test of its accuracy by taking a bearing along a transit, in much the same way as a transit can be used to check the accuracy of a steering compass.

Deviation and Flux Gate Compasses

Flux gate compasses are just as susceptible to deviation as any other magnetic compass. They have the advantage that the sensor can be placed anywhere in the boat, where deviating influences may be less than at the steering position, but this is partly outweighed by the fact that the sensor is usually a small black component, out of sight and out of mind in a locker. It is very easy for anyone unwittingly to place deviating objects close to it without being aware of the consequences.

A major advantage of flux gate compasses is that they almost all include an automatic calibration facility that measures and corrects for deviation automatically. The procedure varies, but usually involves turning the boat slowly through 720°. It is easy, quick and costs nothing, so there is no reason not to do it regularly. Once it has been done, the flux gate's display should show deviation-free magnetic directions – but it is still worth checking by carrying out a conventional compass swing or by spot-checking against any convenient transit.

Combined Compass Errors

The existence of two correctable errors – variation and deviation – mean that we have to get used to dealing with three different kinds of north (Figure 13) and be able to convert directions from one form to another.

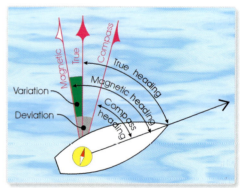

Figure 13

Until recently, most charts showed Magnetic directions as well as True, but this practice is becoming less common. In any case, the most useful ways of expressing direction are 'Compass' (as shown by the boat's compass) and 'True' (referring to the real world and to the parallels and meridians of latitude and longitude shown on the chart).

Magnetic directions are mainly used as a stepping stone in the conversion process from one to the other.

As the arithmetic involved in correcting for variation and deviation is essentially the same, it is quite possible to combine the two. Suppose, for instance, we are steering 150°(C) and need to convert it to True in order to plot it on the chart. Variation (taken from the chart) is 6° W and deviation (taken from the Deviation Card) is 5°E.

The full calculation looks like this:

Compass heading	150° (C)	
Correct for Deviation	+ 5° E	(Add easterly error)
Magnetic heading	155° (M)	
Correct for Variation	- 6° W	(Subtract westerly error)
True Heading	149° (T)	

In this particular example, the end result is a change of only 1 degree, so it hardly seems worth all the effort. It would be easier, quicker, and more reliable if we looked at the two errors, and applied a combined correction, like this:

Westerly error	6°	
Easterly error	5°	
Combined error	1° W	
Compass heading	150° (C)	
Combined correction	- 1° W	(Subtract westerly error)
True Heading	149° (T)	

This method is perfectly acceptable so long as both errors are small – less than about 10°. The stepping-stone analogy is useful: if you were crossing a very small stream, with stepping stones close together, it might be better to cross in a single step rather than risk slipping in the middle.

Coping with Large Errors

If the gaps between the stepping stones are large, however, it is safer to take them one step at a time – and the same is true when dealing with large compass errors.

The reason becomes clear if you think of the situation in northern parts of the USA and Canada, where variation is in the order of 20 degrees. Suppose, for instance, that we need to steer a course of 070°(T), and need to convert it to Compass. Variation (taken from the chart) is 22°W.

The deviation card (Figure 12 on page 21) shows that on a heading of 067½°, the deviation is 2°E. From this, the combined error method of calculation suggests that the compass course should be:

Westerly error	22°	
Easterly error	2°	
Combined error	20° W	
True heading	070° (T)	
Combined correction	+ 20° W	(Add westerly error when going from True to Compass)
Compass Heading	090° (C)	

The trouble is that on a heading of 090°(C) the deviation card shows an error of 4°, not the 2° we have used!

So long as the deviation is generally small, this problem can be prevented simply by doing the calculation in full, step-by-step.

The mnemonics True Virgins Make Dull Companions (TVMDC) and Cadbury's Dairy Milk Very Tasty (CDMVT) may help you remember that Variation (V) separates True (T) and Magnetic (M), and that Deviation (D) separates Magnetic (M) from Compass (C).

If the deviation is also large, the process may warrant a further refinement known as second error correction. In effect, this involves doing the deviation calculation twice. The first time gives an approximate answer, which is then used to make a more accurate estimate of the amount of deviation to apply.

Suppose, for instance, that we need to convert a course of 090°(T) to Compass, in an area where variation (taken from the chart) is 22° W, and on the boat whose deviation card is shown in Figure 14.

True heading	090° (T)
Correct for variation	+ 22° W
Magnetic heading	112° (M)
Correct for deviation	- 18° E
Compass heading	094° (C)

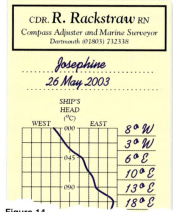

CDR. **R. Rackstraw** RN
Compass Adjuster and Marine Surveyor
Dartmouth (01803) 732338

Josephine
26 May 2003

SHIP'S HEAD (°C)

WEST	EAST	
000		8° W
		3° W
045		6° E
		10° E
090		13° E
		18° E

Figure 14

This first error correction suggests that the deviation is more like 13°E than 18°E. Using this to revise the calculation gives a second error correction result of 099°.

Non-Magnetic Compasses

Variation and deviation are undeniably nuisances. Navigation would be much simpler, more accurate, and less prone to human error if compasses indicated direction relative to True North.

At present there are at least two completely different types of compass available that can do exactly that. They are the gyro compass and the GPS compass. Others, such as ring laser gyros, which are used in military applications and aircraft, may eventually trickle down to recreational craft.

Gyro compasses and GPS compasses are heavy, expensive and dependent on electrical power. Of the two, gyro compasses have been tried, tested and developed for longer, and have the advantage of being completely independent, but they are also the more expensive, and suffer the drawback that they must be switched on several hours before they are required. A gyro compass will usually withstand temporary interruptions to its power supply (though its associated display equipment may not!) but, because it is essentially a mechanical device, its performance will eventually deteriorate as wear and tear take their toll. Accuracy also deteriorates as speed increases, a feature that can be predicted and therefore corrected, but which is inherent in the way the compass works.

GPS compasses are a spin-off from the Global Positioning System (see page 63). At present (2013), they are relatively expensive compared with magnetic compasses, but are cheaper than gyros, and offer similar accuracy without the need for 'running-up' in advance. They have no moving parts so maintenance is minimal, but any failure of the power supply will cause an instant failure of the compass. They are also totally dependent on the Global Positioning System.

How a Gyro Compass Works

The heart of a gyro compass is a heavy metal wheel – typically several kilograms in weight – turning at high speed. This gyroscope has two properties that make it useful as a compass:

- Gyroscopic inertia
- Precession

Gyroscopic inertia means that a gyroscope naturally tries to keep its spin axis pointing in the same direction in space. In other words, if you started it spinning with its axis pointing towards a distant star it would keep tracking the star even while the Earth turned underneath it. If the star happened to be rising over the eastern horizon at the time, the gyro would gradually tilt upwards as the star rose, then turn and tilt downwards again as the star set.

Precession is a curious characteristic of gyroscopes. If you try to divert the axis of the spinning rotor, gyroscopic inertia means that it resists your efforts. Precession, however, means that it will move – albeit slowly – but at right angles to the force you apply.

If the gyroscope is mounted in a ballasted frame then as it tries to tilt to track the star the frame will apply an opposing (downward) force to the eastern end of the shaft. The gyroscope's response is to precess the eastern end of the shaft southward.

This process continues until the gyroscope eventually settles with its shaft aligned with the Earth's axis of spin – pointing True North.

How a GPS Compass Works

A GPS compass consists of two or three antennas – typically small, mushroom-shaped units – mounted on a horizontal bar or tripod mounting and linked to a single processing unit.

The GPS satellites (see page 64) transmit microwaves, with a wavelength of about 20cm. Like all radio waves they are made up of fluctuating electrical and magnetic fields, but it is easier to visualise as though they were ripples on a pond, spreading outwards from the satellite.

If the two antennas are exactly the same distance from a satellite, the processor will receive two copies of the signal – one through each antenna – at precisely the same moment, and perfectly in phase with each other (i.e. with the 'crests' and 'troughs' of the signal arriving at one antenna perfectly in step with those arriving at the other).

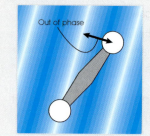

If one antenna is slightly further away from the satellite than the other, however, the central processor will receive two versions of the signal, slightly out of phase with each other. If, for instance, one antenna is receiving the 'crest' of a wave while its twin is receiving the 'trough', then one antenna must be 10cm nearer to the satellite than the other.

The satellite signal includes details of its precise position in space, so the GPS compass knows where the signals are coming from. From the phase difference between the signals received by its two antennas, the compass can also calculate its own orientation relative to the satellite. By combining the two, it can calculate the vessel's heading.

Measuring Direction – on a Paper Chart

Direction, on a chart, is shown in two ways:

- The meridians and parallels that make up the grid of latitude and longitude.
- Compass roses – representations of a compass card, dotted around the chart. All compass roses have a ring of graduations showing directions relative to True North. Some, but not all, have a second, inner ring showing graduations relative to magnetic north at the time the chart was produced. Some older charts have a third ring inside the other two, showing compass points.

Unfortunately, although everyday navigation often involves drawing a line in a particular direction, or measuring the direction of a line that you have just drawn, those lines hardly ever pass through the centre of a compass rose. Literally dozens of different gadgets have been invented to overcome this problem, but they can usefully be divided into four groups:

- Protractors.
- Single-arm plotters.
- Parallel rulers.
- Breton-type plotters.

You don't need to be able to use all of them, but it's essential to be thoroughly familiar with at least one, and useful to be able to manage one or two alternatives in case you ever need to navigate with someone else's choice of equipment.

Protractors

Several types of protractor are sold for chartwork. Their shapes vary from semicircular, like those used in school geometry lessons, through navigational triangles, to squares or rectangles, but essentially they all consist of a flat piece of transparent plastic, marked with a scale of degrees. Most have a small hole at the centre of the scale.

There are two ways of using a protractor, depending mainly on whether the scale of degrees is marked in a clockwise or anticlockwise direction. Some, including the Douglas Protractor and its variants, have two scales running in opposite directions, so you can use either.

To Measure the Direction of an Existing Line using a Clockwise Scale

Put the central hole on the line, preferably where it crosses either a north-south meridian or an east-west parallel of latitude (Figure 15). Line up the grid on the protractor with the meridian or parallel, and read off the direction where the line you are measuring cuts the scale marked on the protractor.

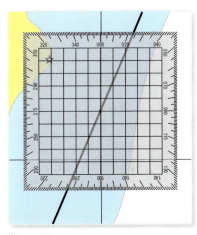

Figure 15

To Draw a Line in a Particular Direction using a Clockwise Scale

Put the central hole of the protractor on the point at which you intend to start the line, and rotate the protractor so that the grid marked on it is parallel to the grid of meridians and parallels on the chart (Figure 16). Make a pencil mark through the central hole, and another one next to the point on the scale that corresponds to the direction you are interested in. Then use a straight edge (either a separate ruler or the edge of the protractor itself) to draw a line passing through the two marks.

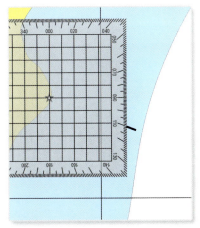

Figure 16

If you want to draw the reciprocal (a line heading in the opposite direction, so that it represents the direction from something rather than the direction to something), it can easily be achieved by exactly the same process, but using the protractor upside down, so that its north mark points south.

To Measure the Direction of an Existing Line using an Anticlockwise Scale

Place the protractor on the chart, with its 000°–180° line (or one of the edges or grid lines that is parallel to it) along the line on the chart (Figure 17). Slide it along the line until its central hole is over a meridian, then read off the direction where the meridian passes through the anticlockwise scale.

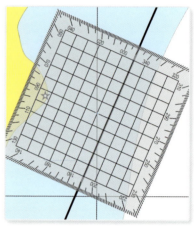

Figure 17

To Draw a Line in a Particular Direction using an Anticlockwise Scale

Place the hole in the centre of the protractor over a suitable meridian, and rotate the protractor until the meridian passes through the appropriate mark on the anticlockwise scale (Figure 18). Keeping this alignment, slide the protractor up or down the meridian until the ruling edge (one that is parallel to its 000°–180° line) passes through the starting point of your intended line. Then use the ruling edge to rule the line.

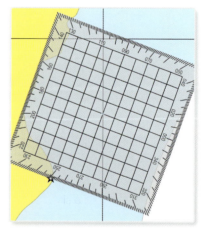

Figure 18

Parallel Rulers

Parallel rulers (Figure 19), consisting of two straight rulers held together by a linkage that keeps them parallel to each other but allows them to move closer together or further apart, are the traditional tool for measuring and plotting courses, tracks and bearings. Originally, they achieved this by being lined up with a compass rose printed on the chart, and then 'walking' to wherever the course, track or bearing was to be drawn. Measuring the direction of a line was the reverse: the parallels had to be lined up with the line in question, and then walked to the nearest compass rose.

Figure 19

This business of walking across the chart gave them a bad name – and justifiably so. On a large, stable platform they were fine. On a small, bouncing, jolting chart table, they tended to slip, particularly if the linkages were stiff.

A later variation consisted of a single, much wider ruler, with a roller set into each end. The two rollers were linked by a shaft, so if one end rolled forward, the other end had to roll forwards exactly the same distance, so the ruler kept its orientation as it was rolled around the chart. The trouble with such 'rolling parallels' is that they need a big chart table that is perfectly flat.

Now, however, clear acrylic has replaced the brass and boxwood rulers of old, and Captain Fields' markings – or markings very similar to them – are virtually standard.

Captain Fields' markings (as seen in Figure 19) are simply a protractor, printed or engraved on the parallel ruler to free it from the tyranny of the printed compass rose. It works like any other anticlockwise protractor – with the proviso that it must be in its 'closed' position and bearing in mind that the centre of the scale is actually in the middle of one of the long edges.

To Measure the Direction of an Existing Line

Place the parallel rulers on the chart, with one edge touching the line (Figure 19).

Holding the upper ruler (the one with most of the numbers on it) in place by pressing it firmly down onto the chart, swing the other ruler around until the centre mark (often labelled 'S') is touching one of the meridians marked on the chart (Figure 20).

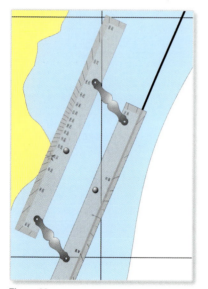

Figure 20

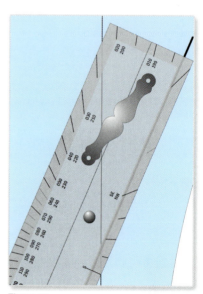

Figure 21

Holding that ruler in place, move the upper ruler into its 'shut' position. Read off the direction where the meridian passes through the scale marked on the ruler (Figure 21).

To Draw a Line in a Particular Direction

Place the rulers on the chart in roughly the right place. Keeping the two rulers together, place the centre mark (often labelled 'S') so that its tip is just touching one of the meridians marked on the chart, and rotate the rulers until the meridian passes through the appropriate mark on the scale. Holding one ruler in place by pressing it firmly down onto the chart, move the other ruler to where the line is to be drawn.

Single-Arm Plotters

The principle of a single arm plotter is simple: it's a portable compass rose that can be placed on the chart wherever it is required and has a ruler that is free to rotate around the centre of the scale. The base-plate is marked with a rectangular grid so that it can be accurately lined up with the meridians and parallels on the chart (Figure 22). On some versions, the scale of degrees can be rotated separately, allowing it to be offset to show Magnetic directions instead of True.

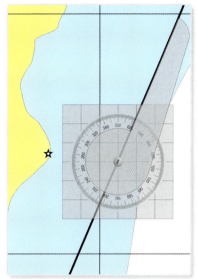

Figure 22

Breton-Type Plotters

The term Breton Plotter is a registered trademark that refers to a plotting instrument invented in the 1960s by a French navigation instructor called Yvonnick Gueret that has been much copied and adapted since.

The standard features of a Breton-type plotter are a rectangular base plate with a circular protractor mounted on top of it but free to rotate. A grid of squares on the protractor is used to line it up with the chart.

To Measure the Direction of a Line

Lay one edge of the base plate along the line in question and rotate the protractor until its grid lines up with the meridians and parallels on the chart (Figure 23). Then read off the True bearing from where the centreline of the base plate meets the edge of the protractor (Figure 24).

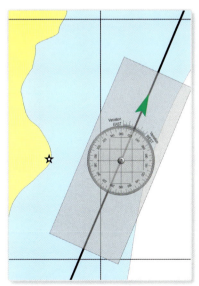

Figure 23

To Draw a Line in a Particular Direction

Rotate the protractor so that the required direction is lined up with the centreline of the base plate, then position the whole plotter on the chart, with one of its edges touching the starting point of the intended line, and adjust its position until the protractor grid lines up with the parallels and meridians.

An extra refinement that has undoubtedly done a lot to make the Breton-type plotter so popular is that if you prefer to work in Magnetic you can easily do so simply by reading off bearings or setting courses against the relevant part of the variation scale marked on the base plate, rather than against the centreline.

Figure 24

Summary

- Directions are usually given as angles, measured clockwise from North (000°).
- On charts, direction is indicated by the grid of meridians and parallels, and by circular compass roses.
- In the real world, direction is measured by compasses.
  - Most small craft use compasses that work by sensing the direction of the Earth's magnetic field.

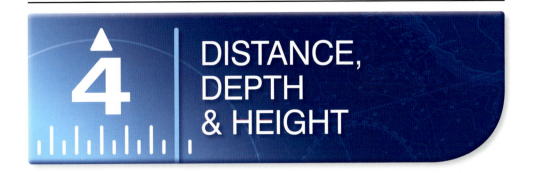

4 DISTANCE, DEPTH & HEIGHT

Like direction, our measurements of distance are also related to the invisible graticule of meridians and parallels that covers the Earth.

A sea mile is defined as the length of 1 minute of arc (one-sixtieth of a degree) measured along a meridian at the Earth's surface. Unfortunately, as the Earth is not a perfect sphere, this means that the length of a sea mile varies slightly, from about 1,842.9 metres at the Equator to 1,861.7 metres at the poles. Even these measurements vary slightly, depending which definition of the shape of the Earth you happen to be using (see page 9 – Horizontal Datums)!

A unit of distance that varies from place to place is obviously less than ideal so, by international agreement, a nautical mile is defined as exactly 1,852 metres – the average length of a sea mile, rounded down to the nearest whole metre.

For practical navigation, the difference between a sea mile and a nautical mile is so slight that it can almost always be ignored, so in practice the latitude scale on a chart also serves as the scale of distance.

The meridians converge towards the poles, so the distance represented by a minute of longitude varies from about 1,855 metres at the Equator to zero at the poles.[2] This means that a minute of longitude is useless as a measure of distance.

The statute mile is a distance of 1,760 yards or 5,280 feet (approximately 1,609.3 metres). It is not an international unit, and is never used in marine navigation.

A metre is the international standard unit of distance. Like the sea mile, it was originally based on the size of the Earth, as it was defined as one ten-millionth of the distance from the Equator to the North Pole, measured through Paris. It has been redefined several times since, and is now officially defined as 'the length of the path travelled by light in a vacuum during a time interval of 1/299,792,458 of a second'.

It is used for measuring short distances at sea, and for measuring heights and depths.

A thousand metres are a kilometre. Kilometres are sometimes used on inland waterways, especially in mainland Europe, but are never used in marine navigation.

---

[2] An approximate formula for converting minutes of longitude to nautical miles is *dLong x cos Lat = distance*. The distance in minutes of Longitude is dLong and cos Lat is the cosine of the Latitude. At 50°N (e.g. Scilly Isles), 1 minute of longitude = 1190m. At 60°N (e.g. Shetland), 1 minutes of longitude = 926m.

Obsolete Units

A number of obsolete units are still used informally, for approximate measurements, and will be found in old books and publications:

- A foot is approximately 30 centimetres. It is still used in the USA, particularly for measurements of height and depth.
- A yard is 3 feet or 0.914m.
- A fathom is 6 feet – used mainly for measurements of depth.
- A cable is a tenth of a nautical mile. It is approximately 200 yards or 100 fathoms, and is occasionally used for approximate measurements of short distances.

Speed

Speed, at sea, is usually measured in knots, except in a few specialised situations such as waterskiing and powerboat racing. A knot is 1 nautical mile per hour. A common beginners' mistake is to talk about 'knots per hour'. This is meaningless, except in the unlikely situation in which it could be used as a measure of acceleration.

Measuring Distance – in the Real World

Perhaps the most important distance to measure, for navigational purposes, is the distance a boat has moved.

It's generally impractical to measure this directly. It's relatively easy, however, to measure the distance a vessel has moved through the water. If it takes 3 seconds, for instance, for a 10-metre boat to sail past a piece of floating weed, then the boat must be moving at 10 metres per 3 seconds, or 200 metres per minute, or about 12,000 metres per hour (about 6.5 knots). A variation of this idea was probably used by Columbus and Magellan, in which a block of wood was dropped over the stern of a ship, attached to a long length of line marked by knots at regular intervals. Speed was measured by counting the number of knots that were dragged overboard in a given time as the ship sailed away from the block of wood. This is why speed is measured in knots, and is probably why the instrument which does the measuring is called a 'log'.

A more refined log was invented almost 150 years ago. Often called the Walker log, after its inventor, the taffrail log or trailing log is no longer in production, but there are still plenty of them around and in use. There are several different makes and models, but they all consist of a cigar-shaped spinner with spiral fins that is towed astern on a long length of braided line. As it is dragged through the water, the spinner spins, twisting the line. As the line twists it turns a shaft at the back of the display unit, which is clamped to the taffrail (stern) of the boat. Inside the display unit a reduction gearbox reduces the rapidly spinning motion of the input shaft to a very slow movement of the hands on a dial to show the distance travelled.

The mechanical taffrail log is inherently reliable, easy to look after and remarkably accurate at speeds between about 2 and 10 knots. However, it doesn't work at very high or low speeds and is a nuisance to stream and recover. The logical progression was to use a similar (but smaller) impeller attached directly to the hull, with an electronic sensor to count the number of revolutions.

That, too, has been superseded, and almost all logs now use a paddlewheel, typically about 2–3cm in diameter. The paddlewheel has a small magnet mounted in one of its blades and is mounted in a cylindrical probe, called a transducer, that passes down through a tube set into the bottom of the boat. The principle, however, is the same: by counting the revolutions of the paddlewheel the log can measure the speed of the boat and the distance it has travelled.

Even this is far from perfect, mainly because the paddlewheel is very susceptible to the slightest fouling or to physical damage.

Some high-performance boats (especially ski-boats and similar small powerboats) use a pitot log, which works by measuring the pressure exerted by the water on the forward face of a tubular sensor. Such logs are compact, cheap, and reasonably reliable, but are usually incapable of reading speeds below about ten knots, and seldom include a distance-measuring facility.

An electromagnetic log uses an electromagnet to create a fluctuating magnetic field around its transducer. As the water flows past the transducer the magnetic field generates a voltage in the water, just as the magnets of a car's alternator generate a voltage in its wires that can be used to charge the battery. In the case of an electromagnetic log the voltage is very much lower, but it increases as the boat speed increases so it can be measured by a probe in the transducer to give an indication of speed. Electromagnetic logs are reliable and accurate, but are very bulky and expensive, and use more power than most others, so their use is generally confined to commercial vessels and large motor-yachts.

At least two types of sonic logs use sound waves. One type has two transducers mounted a few centimetres (or in some cases a few metres) apart. Each transducer produces a sequence of high-frequency sound pulses ('clicks'), which are detected by the other. When the boat is stationary it takes just as long for a click to travel from the aft transducer to the forward one as it does for the click travelling the other way to go from forward to aft. As the boat starts moving, however, the time taken by the aft-going click to complete its journey reduces, while the forward-going click takes longer. By comparing the two, the log can calculate how fast the boat is moving.

Another version uses a single transducer. It works by transmitting high-frequency clicks and listening for the echoes received as they bounce back from particles of dirt or plankton in the water. When the boat is moving, particles approaching the transducer produce higher-frequency echoes than those moving away from it. By comparing the two frequencies against the frequency it transmitted, the log can work out the boat speed.

Log Errors

No log can be expected to be 100 per cent accurate. The boat may drag some water along with it, making the water's flow past its transducer slightly less than the boat's speed through the water, or the impeller itself may not be spinning freely. Alternatively, the water's flow may be accelerated as it passes the keel or is sucked into the propellers, making the log over-read.

The process of measuring and correcting log error is known as calibration, and involves measuring the time the boat takes to cover a known distance and using this to calculate the true speed, which can be compared with the speed shown by the log.

The best distances to use are the measured distances that have been set up especially for the purpose in, or close to, many major ports and harbours, marked with transit posts. The distance and the course to steer are shown on the chart. There's no reason, though, why you shouldn't use any distance that you can measure accurately on the chart. Last, but by no means least, you can use the speed shown by a GPS set. It's important to appreciate, though, that all these techniques measure the speed over the ground, rather than the speed through the water that is measured by the log. To overcome this problem, calibration runs need to be carried out in two opposite directions.

Choose a reasonably calm day, ideally at a time and place where the tidal stream is weak. Under power, settle the boat onto the required course well before you reach the beginning of the measured distance in order to let the speed settle, and then hold that course and speed until you reach the end. Record the time at which you cross the start line and finish line and keep a note of the actual log reading during the run.

Then repeat the process, at the same log speed, in the opposite direction.

Work out your average speed on each run and then work out the average of the two speeds. It's important not to try to shorten the process by adding the times together and dividing the distance by that, because you will get a different answer.

Compare your averaged speed with the speed shown by the log to find the log error, and consult the equipment instructions to find out how to correct it. A single pair of calibration runs is better than nothing, but ideally you should carry out at least four, at each of several representative speeds.

The calculation looks like this:

Measured distance	1,852m (1.00 nautical mile)
Time (north-bound run)	4 min 38 sec = 278 sec = 0.07722 hours
Speed (over ground)	12.95 knots
Log speed	13.1 knots
Time (southbound run)	5min 17 sec = 317 sec = 0.08805 hours
Speed (over ground)	11.36 knots
Log speed	13.2 knots
Average speed over ground	12.16 knots
Average log speed	13.15 knots
Discrepancy	1.01 knots
Log over-reads by	7.7 per cent

Measuring Distance – on a Paper Chart

For almost all practical purposes, the latitude scale on the side of a paper chart serves as the scale of distance (Figure 25). It's extremely unusual, though, to want to measure distances directly north or south. More often, we need to measure the distance between two points in some completely different direction, or draw a line of a particular length – such as to represent the distance a boat has travelled.

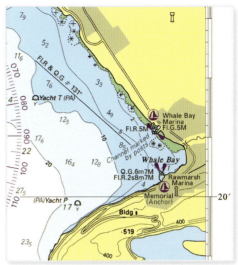

Figure 25

Dividers

The usual tool for the job is a pair of dividers.

For classroom navigation, the kind that are used for technical drawing are fine: their needle-sharp points give a reassuring sense of precision, particularly if they are opened and closed by a screw mechanism. They tend to be small, fragile and rather awkward for practical navigation at sea, though, so it is better to use a pair of dividers that has been made for the job.

There are two common types, both available in a range of sizes. Straight dividers have straight legs, opened and closed simply by pulling the points apart or pushing them together. Single-handed or bow dividers have a semicircular bend at the top of each leg, so that when they are in their closed position the two bends form a circle. Squeezing the circle between your thumb and your first and second fingers makes the legs cross and the points move further apart. Squeezing the straight part of the legs, between the ball of your thumb and ring and little fingers, moves the points closer together. The technique seems clumsy at first but soon becomes second nature, and allows the dividers to be opened and closed quickly with one hand, leaving the other free to wield a pencil.

Compasses

For some purposes, such as plotting fixes based on radar ranges (see page 170), marking the visible range of a light (see page 82) or drawing a spider's web or ladder for rapid plotting (see pages 72–73), a pair of drawing compasses is useful. Large brass ones are available, with a clamp to take a pencil, but on most yachts and motor boats the compasses are unlikely to see as much use as dividers, so a cheap pair from a school geometry set is likely to be adequate. The types used for technical drawing are less suitable, because they usually have very hard leads.

Distortion of Latitude

Whatever tool you are using to transfer distances between the latitude scale and the part of the chart you are working on, it is worth bearing in mind that the flat chart is a slightly distorted representation of the curved surface of the Earth (see page 7). Over very short distances the effect is negligible, so on large-scale charts such as harbour plans it can be ignored.

On small-scale charts, such as those covering areas larger than about 1 degree of latitude (60 miles) from top to bottom, it starts to become noticeable that 1 minute of latitude measured at the upper end of the latitude scale is not represented by the same distance as a minute of latitude at the bottom.

Except on very small-scale charts, such as those which might be used for planning a complete cruise, the difference is small compared with the other errors that we have to contend with, but its effects can be eliminated altogether by using the section of the latitude scale that is at least roughly level with the distance you are measuring.

Using Direction and Distance to Express Position

Combining direction and distance is a very useful and intuitive way of expressing position, such as 'Sark is about six miles east of Guernsey'.

It can be very precise, as in 'Cathead buoy is 341.0°T x 2,743 metres from Calshot radar scanner'.

Some care is needed, though, because the format used can vary between different applications. GPS sets, for instance, usually give the bearing to a waypoint, so a yacht approaching Plymouth might see the range and bearing of the breakwater light given as 3.7 miles, 032°.

Reporting to the Coastguard, however, her position should be given from the reference point:

"My position from Plymouth Breakwater light is 212 degrees, 3.7 miles."

Imagine you are giving directions to a helicopter pilot:

- First, he needs to know where to start from…
- …then which direction to set off in…
- …and finally, when to stop.

Although the position is the same, the order in which the information is given is different, and the direction is reversed.

Depth and Height

If a notice on the side of a swimming pool says the water is 1.3m deep, it's fair to assume that it will be about chest high on an adult standing on the bottom. It doesn't matter whether the swimming pool is on a hill or in a valley, or even on board a ship.

That, however, is a very simple situation. In navigation we are dealing with a surface that moves up and down and with objects that may move with the surface, such as our own boats, buoys and lightships, or that may be fixed to the Earth's crust, such as the sea bed, rocks and lighthouses.

Dealing with depths and heights is not really difficult, so long as you bear in mind that there are four different levels from which things are often measured:

- Actual sea level.
- Mean High Water Springs.
- Highest Astronomical Tide.
- Chart datum.

You are quite likely to come across two others, of more academic interest:

- Mean Sea Level or the Geoid.
- The Spheroid.

The Geoid

The term Mean Sea Level is almost self-explanatory: it's the mean level of the sea, averaging out the effect of tides. It is not used for marine navigation, but is the level against which heights are shown on many land maps. The concept of there being a sea level at somewhere such as Coventry (or even Tibet!), is somewhat bizarre, but it is really only a colloquial expression for what is technically known as the geoid. The geoid is defined as the equipotential surface of the Earth's gravitational field: in simple terms it is the surface that appears to be 'horizontal' wherever you happen to be in the world. Because the Earth is not a uniform lump of rock its gravitational field varies from place to place, so the geoid is not a neat geometrical shape. It ranges from over 100m below the WGS spheroid in the Indian Ocean to nearly 80m above it in the western Pacific.

The Spheroid

Accurate map-making and satellite positioning rely on neat, consistent and reasonably simple mathematical models of the Earth as their foundations. These smooth, symmetrical models are known as spheroids. There are several different spheroids in use, contributing to the discrepancies between different horizontal datums (see page 9). So far as heights and depths are concerned, however, they are important only because when a GPS receiver shows height or altitude it is referring to height above (or below) the spheroid. Around the UK, the geoid (Mean Sea Level) is about 50m above the spheroid.

Actual sea level is self-explanatory: it's the level of the sea at any given moment, averaged out to remove the effect of waves. It's the reference against which you know the depth of your boat's keel or propellers, the height of your mast or superstructure, and against which the charted height of floating structures such as lightships are given.

Mean High Water Springs (MHWS) is the level against which the height of things such as lighthouses and islands are mentioned – anything which is almost always above water. Sea level rises and falls according to a regular pattern, rising to High Water (HW), then falling to Low Water (LW) about six hours later, before rising again. This daily pattern, however, is overlaid on a slower pattern, in which tides with very high High Waters and very low Low Waters are interspersed by tides in which the difference is much less pronounced. The small (Neap) tides happen about a week before and after the big (Spring) tides. Mean High Water Springs is the average level reached by High Water over a succession of spring tides.

In general, using MHWS gives a somewhat pessimistic value of the height of something; lighthouses are usually higher above actual sea level than is shown on the chart. Remember, though, that MHWS is based on an average spring tide; there are times, especially in Spring and Autumn, where actual sea level rises above MHWS.

Highest Astronomical Tide is being introduced as the level from which the vertical clearance under overhead obstructions such as bridges and power cables is measured. As the name suggests, it is the highest level to which the tide is ever expected to rise, intended to give the most pessimistic figure for the headroom available under an obstruction, but it is still possible that, on rare occasions, exceptional meteorological conditions may cause the sea level to rise above HAT.

Chart datum is the level used to indicate the depth of the sea bed and the height of things that are regularly covered and uncovered by the sea as it rises and falls. This includes all the most dangerous rocks and sandbanks, which are close to the surface but often hidden.

In theory, it is the lowest level to which the tide is ever expected to fall, so as to give the most pessimistic figure for the actual depth of water. It is almost completely safe to assume that there is more water than is shown on the chart. On very rare occasions the tide may fall lower than was predicted when Chart Datum was set, or meteorological factors such as high barometric pressure push the actual sea level down.

Charted Depths

On a chart, depths and heights can be shown in two main ways:

- Spot depths (and heights).
- Contours.

The depth below chart datum of a particular point on the sea bed can be shown by a number, such as the '27_5' in the left centre of the chart extract (Figure 26). This is called a spot depth or sounding, and in this particular instance indicates that there is a depth of 27.5 metres plus the height of tide.

Contour lines join points that are of equal depth. The wriggling line that separates the white and blue areas in the lower half of

Figure 26

the chart extract, for instance, is the 20-metre contour. In this particular case, a difference in colour is used to draw attention to the contour line, but that is not always the case, nor is the 20-metre contour always among those picked out for such special attention. In general, though, colouring follows the principle that white areas are deeper than blue ones, and light blue is deeper than darker blue.

Contour lines and their associated colouring give useful information about the shape of the sea bed. Widely spaced contours mean that there is little change in depth over wide areas; the sea bed, in other words, is reasonably smooth. Where contours are packed close together, it indicates dramatic changes of depth over short distances, implying a rough or steeply shelving bottom.

Circular contours (such as the one surrounding the '30' in the bottom left-hand corner of the chart extract) represent either deeper pools or isolated shallow patches, depending on whether the depth in the middle of the circle is more or less than those surrounding it.

One contour that is of particular importance is the 0-metre contour or drying line, so called because anything above the drying line is sometimes uncovered by the receding tide. These drying areas are invariably coloured green on British Admiralty charts. There may be spot depths shown for things that are above the drying line, except that they are then called drying heights instead of soundings. The most obvious indication that something is a drying height rather than a sounding, of course, is that it relates to a green area on the chart, but that isn't always possible. Towards the bottom right-hand corner of the chart extract, for instance, is a drying rock indicated by an asterisk (Warsash Rock). It's too small to be shown as a patch of green but its drying height is shown as 04 (0.4 metres). The underlining shows that it's a drying height, or you could think of it as a subtraction sign, indicating that it's a negative sounding – one that goes upwards from chart datum instead of downwards.

In the large green area at the top of Figure 26 there's a rocky ledge, with several examples of another type of height, such as the '(43)' alongside the Weyman Islands. The brackets indicate that it is out of context from the surrounding colour, but its other key feature is that it is not underlined, so it is not a drying height but a charted height or elevation. In other words, it refers to something that is not routinely covered and uncovered by the tide, but which stands 43 metres above Mean High Water Springs.

Areas above MHWS that are large enough to be coloured appear yellow on British Admiralty charts. Contours and spot heights indicate the shape of the land, just as contours and soundings indicate the shape of the sea bed, except that they too are shown relative to MHWS.

Measuring Depth – in the Real World

At low speeds, and in very shallow water, it's perfectly possible to measure depth with a stick, such as the handle of a boathook, marked off in tenths of a metre. In slightly deeper water a weight on the end of a piece of string can be used – a lead and line. Until about 1935 even survey ships used this method, and it was standard practice on yachts right up to the 1950s and 1960s. It's awkward and tedious, though, and becomes increasingly difficult and unreliable as the speed or depth increase, so the lead and line was one of the first traditional navigation tools to be replaced by electronics, in the shape of an echo sounder.

How an Echo Sounder Works

An echo sounder works by transmitting very short pulses of high-frequency sound that travel down to the sea bed and are reflected back to the transducer. The speed of sound in sea water varies slightly but is always in the order of 1,400 metres per second, so the time taken for a pulse to complete its down-and-back trip depends on the depth of water. If the echo is received 0.01 seconds after the pulse was transmitted, for instance, the pulse must have travelled a total of 14 metres, meaning that the sea bed must be 7 metres from the transducer.

Most early echo sounders had what were known as 'flasher' or 'rotating neon' displays, which used a fast-spinning rotor with a small neon lamp or light-emitting diode at one end. Each time the rotor passed the upright position the light or diode flashed and the transducer was triggered to transmit its pulse. When the returning echo was received, the light flashed again. By that time, the spinning arm had moved on. How far it moved depended on the time interval between transmission and reception, so the depth of water was indicated by the position of the second flash, and could be read directly from a scale marked on the face of the instrument.

Some people still prefer flasher sounders because, with practice, it's possible to make an informed guess about the quality of the sea bed by looking at the nature of the return flash: a bright, compact flash suggests a hard bottom such as firm sand or rock, while a weaker, more drawn-out flash implies a softer bottom such as mud.

Most echo sounders, however, use an electronic display, showing the depth either as numbers or – in 'fish finders' – as a continuously updated graph.

Digital Echo Sounders

To produce a simple digital display of depth an echo sounder has to overcome a number of problems, and has to include computer software capable of making a number of informed decisions.

Air bubbles, for instance, are good reflectors of sound waves in water. Fish-finders use this principle: they work by detecting the pocket of air trapped inside a fish's swim bladder. For navigation purposes it's a nuisance: fish, or the propeller wash of other boats, can easily produce strong echoes at much shallower depths than the real sea bed.

The echo sounder can't, however, assume that the deepest echo is the real one. In very shallow water, or over a rocky sea bed, it is quite possible for the returning echo to bounce back from the hull of the boat or from the sea surface and set off on another down-and-back trip.

In deep water and with a hard bottom, the echo from one pulse may not return until after another pulse has been sent. On a flasher sounder set to an operating range of 0–12 metres, 15 metres of water would give an indicated depth of 3 metres, but the problem can easily be resolved by switching up to a deeper operating range, with longer intervals between the pulses.

Digital or graphical sounders have to do much the same. If you listen to the clicks produced by a modern sounder's transducer you are likely to find that they don't occur at regular intervals, as you might expect, but that a string of closely spaced clicks are interspersed by two or three at rather longer intervals as the echo sounder checks up to make sure that it isn't being misled by these second trace echoes.

Using an Echo Sounder

Measuring the depth with an old-fashioned echo sounder is simple. You just turn it on, set it to whichever range scale is most appropriate for the depth of water you are operating in, and adjust the 'gain' control to the lowest setting at which the unit still shows a solid, consistent display of depth. Using a modern digital instrument is even easier: in most cases, all you need to do is turn it on!

Bear in mind that, when it leaves the factory an echo sounder will almost invariably be set up to show the depth below the transducer – not the actual depth of water from the surface to the bottom, or the depth below the keel. Most allow you to adjust the displayed depth by a few feet in either direction, so you can set your echo sounder to display whichever of these two you prefer. Depth below the keel errs on the side of pessimism, but depth below the surface is generally more useful for navigational purposes.

One other significant feature of most modern echo sounders is an alarm which can be set to go off if the depth is shallower or deeper than a pre-set level. A shallow alarm is of obvious value if you are operating short-handed in shoal water, because it saves you having to keep one eye on the echo sounder display. A deep alarm can be useful at anchor, when it can be set to serve as a reminder to let out more cable as the tide rises. Used together, the shallow and deep alarms can be useful in fog, or when trying to grope your way up a poorly marked channel by following depth contours.

The Navigator's Tool Kit

Most navigators, even if they don't own a boat but rely on friends or charter, prefer to use their own tools: by taking their own 'toolkit' they know that they will have all they need, and that they are familiar with its use. What to include and what to leave out is, to some extent, a matter of personal preference – and obviously excludes instruments that are screwed to the boat, such as a steering compass, log and echo sounder.

The following list could be regarded as high priority:

- A plotter – such as a Breton-type plotter, parallel rulers, or protractor, according to preference.
- A pair of dividers – 6-inch/150mm is about the smallest practical size. Very large ones are quicker to use but more difficult to adjust with any precision. Seven to eight inches (180mm–200mm) is a popular compromise.
- A pencil – avoid the hard pencils favoured for technical drawing or the standard HB pencils: they produce faint lines and dig grooves in the chart. A soft 'artist's' pencil is better: 2B is the norm for chartwork. Mechanical pencils are ideal, so long as you have a supply of suitable leads; if not, you will need…
- A pencil sharpener – ideally one built into a pot to catch the shavings.
- A rubber – like the pencil, this should be soft.

Lower priority, and generally more expensive items which are often regarded as part of a boat's normal equipment, include:

- A hand-bearing compass.
- A hand-held GPS set.
- A pair of binoculars.
- Drawing compasses.

Using the Information – Dead Reckoning

Just before five in the afternoon of 12 July, *Proud Maiden* leaves her berth at Quarry Marina and heads out under the bridge, intending to pass round the northern end of Douglas Island and Webb Ellis Island to reach Endal Marina (see Figure 27).

Figure 27

Looking at the distance from the green buoy FC3 at the mouth of Rampton Bay to the red buoy FC6, and comparing it with the latitude scale printed on the side of the chart, her skipper can see that it's about four miles, and his plotting instrument shows that the bearing of the red buoy from the green one is 307°(T).

Knowing that *Proud Maiden* will make about five knots, he confidently expects to be arriving at Endal before 1900hrs.

Using the CadET rule (see page 17) he converts the bearing of 307°(T) to a compass bearing:

$$
\begin{array}{ll}
307° \text{ (T)} & \\
+\ 7°\ \text{W} & \text{Variation, from the chart} \\
\hline
314° \text{ (M)} & \\
+\ 6°\ \text{W} & \text{Deviation, from the deviation card} \\
\hline
320° \text{ (C)} & \\
\end{array}
$$

At 1710hrs, *Proud Maiden* passes the green buoy. Her skipper alters course to 320°(C), and notes that the log is reading 194.3.

Passing close to an identifiable charted object is one of the best possible ways of knowing where you are – of 'fixing your position' – so it can be marked on the chart with the conventional symbol for a fix: a circle and the time. It's a good idea to give an indication of the direction the boat is moving by drawing a line in the direction of her course.

After half an hour, her skipper notes the log reading again, and sees that it has increased to 196.7, showing that the boat has moved 2.4 miles. If he has moved 2.4 miles in a direction of 307°(T) since passing the buoy, it would seem reasonable to expect that his position should be:

> from the buoy 307°(T); 2.4 miles.

It's easy to mark that position, simply by using dividers to step off the distance along the course line.

- A position based solely on the course and distance travelled through the water since the last known position is known as a dead reckoning position, or DR.
- A DR is usually represented as a cross or 'tick' across the course line, and the time.

Judging by the DR, *Proud Maiden's* crew doesn't really expect to see the buoy just yet, as it should still be a couple of miles away. But there's a buoy much closer than that, barely half a mile away off the port bow. There's something funny about the depth, too. It was almost Low Water when they left the marina, and in this area that means there might be a metre or two more water than is shown on the chart. But instead of showing depths of forty-something metres – as one would expect from the soundings around the DR position – the echo sounder is showing depths of more than 50 metres.

This combination of seeing something unexpected and an echo sounder reading that is not what it should be is a very strong indication that there is something wrong with the 1740 position.

The skipper's suspicions are confirmed when he plots the position shown by his GPS, which says they are at 46° 13'.7N 5° 43'.1W – about a mile south of his DR.

Why this has happened, what to do about it, and how to stop it happening, are covered in the following chapters.

Summary

Distance
- Distances at sea are usually measured in nautical miles (M) and metres (m).
- 1M = 1852m. It is approximately the length of one minute of latitude.
  - The latitude scale on the side of the chart is a scale of distance.

Depth and Height
- Actual sea level rises and falls, so the depths and heights of things shown on charts must be referred to some fixed level.
  - Highest Astronomical Tide is the highest level the sea is predicted to reach (though it may go higher in exceptional conditions).
  - Mean High Water Springs is the level of an average spring tide.
  - Chart datum is generally the level of the Lowest Astronomical Tide.
  - Depths on charts are shown by contour lines, colouring, and 'spot depths'.

Dead Reckoning
- A dead reckoning position is based on distance and direction travelled through the water from a known position, and nothing else.

5 | CHARTS

The very earliest navigators probably relied almost exclusively on local knowledge. When they sailed out of their home waters they simply bought (or battered!) the information they needed out of some passing local.

That ancient technique survives even now. Ships often employ a local pilot to guide them in and out of harbour. Eventually, though, someone must have realised that information such as 'there are rocks up to half a mile off the headland', was a valuable commodity, which could be stored simply by writing it down and then sold. Then, they must have found that drawings and diagrams were often more useful than mere words. Finally, when the compass came along, they were able to combine their illustrated notes and diagrams to produce what we now know as maps or charts.

Chart Suppliers

Most maritime countries, including Britain, have a government department that is responsible for compiling and publishing official charts. In the UK, it is the UK Hydrographic Office (UKHO), which sells its products under the brand name 'Admiralty Charts and Publications'.

The UKHO produces over 3,000 'standard' Admiralty charts, covering UK and some Commonwealth waters in detail and with reduced coverage elsewhere.

It also produces two separate series of charts intended specifically for yachts and small craft:

- Leisure Folios are packs of about a dozen A2 sheets, compiled from Admiralty standard charts but not replicas of them, covering popular waters and adapted to suit small craft.

Some civilian commercial companies also publish charts, using data derived from many different sources (including UKHO).

In the UK, the two main ones are:

- Imray, Laurie, Norie & Wilson, whose Imray charts provide extensive coverage of UK waters and other areas such as the Caribbean and Mediterranean.
- Stanford's charts cover mainly the southern half of Britain and the adjoining European coasts, but are very competitively priced and are printed on synthetic paper that is waterproof and very difficult to tear.

- A map is a diagrammatic representation of a part of the Earth's surface.
- A chart is a map designed to aid navigation at sea or in the air.

In particular, any chart is expected to fulfil three main functions:

- A source of information.
- A work-sheet for calculations.
- A temporary record of navigational events.

Projections

One of the biggest problems facing anyone who wants to produce a map or chart is posed by the fact that the Earth's surface is not flat. Even if we ignore hills and valleys, it is impossible to represent its curved surface on a flat surface without introducing some kind of distortion, just as it is impossible to flatten out the peeled skin of an orange without tearing it, or to wrap a flat sheet of paper snugly around a ball.

There are many different ways of representing a curved surface on a flat one. These are known as projections and each has its own characteristic set of distortions. Which projection is used depends mainly on which type of distortion is least unacceptable in the finished map.

On a map of the world in a school atlas, for instance, the most important feature might be that the areas of different countries are accurately represented. To achieve this, the cartographer could choose a projection such as Mollweide's (Figure 28).

For navigational purposes, however, Mollweide's projection is almost useless because it distorts direction to an unacceptable extent: look how seldom the meridians and parallels appear to intersect at 90 degrees.

Figure 28

Mercator's Projection

One projection is particularly good at representing direction. It's known as Mercator's projection, from the Latinised name of the 16th-century Belgian who invented it. Strictly speaking, Mercator's projection – like Mollweide's – is a purely mathematical concept, but it's easiest to visualise it as the image that would be cast on a sheet of paper wrapped around a globe, with a bright light at the centre (Figure 29).

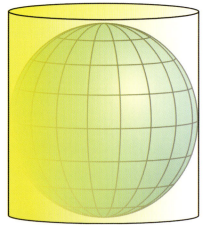

Figure 29

The effect is to make meridians appear as vertical parallel lines, with parallels of latitude as horizontal parallel lines, all intersecting the meridians at exactly 90 degrees.

Distances, however, are distorted, particularly towards the poles, where the meridians on the real world converge and eventually meet. On a Mercator chart, the meridians never meet, so east-west distances near the poles are exaggerated.

Rhumb Lines and Great Circles

The shortest distance between two points is not necessarily a straight line. If you were to take an elastic band and stretch it between two points on the surface of a globe, it would naturally try to contract, and by doing so would show the shortest possible route.

This is called a great circle route, because it lies along the circumference of a circle whose centre is the centre of the Earth. If one point were directly south of the other, it would lie along a meridian (because the meridians themselves are great circles), but if they were due east or west of each other it would not lie along a parallel of latitude, but would appear to bulge away from the Equator and cross every meridian at a slightly different angle. Following a great circle route, in other words, involves progressively altering course as you progress from east to west or vice versa.

If, instead, you were to draw a straight line on a Mercator chart, it would cut every meridian at the same angle, to represent a longer constant-course route known as the rhumb line.

To preserve the shape of land masses, Mercator's projection needs to stretch the latitude scale by exactly the same amount.[3] This is why the parallels of latitude on a Mercator chart are not equally spaced, but are moved further apart nearer the poles (see Distortion of Latitude on page 38).

This means that the scale of a chart changes slightly from top to bottom. For most practical purposes, the effect is barely noticeable, but around the UK it starts to become apparent on charts that cover more than about 60–100 miles from top to bottom. The effect is more serious in higher latitudes, and the North Pole itself can't be shown on any Mercator chart, because the charted meridians can't all pass through a single point.

[3] If Mercator charts were really produced by wrapping sheets of paper around a globe, north-south distances would actually be stretched too much to represent directions accurately. The 'globe wrapped in paper' idea is only a simple analogy for a more complex mathematical principle.

Scale

Scale refers to the relationship between distance on a map and the distance it represents in the real world. If 1cm on a road map represents 2km in the real world, for instance, distances on the map are 1/200,000 as big as they are in the real world, and the map could be described as being at a scale of 1:200,000.

If 10cm represents 1km, it would show considerably more detail, but you would need a huge piece of paper to show even a short journey. Its scale would be 1:10,000.

For this reason, charts are drawn on many different scales:

Large-scale charts, typically at scales of between 1:5,000 and 1:25,000, are used for harbour plans and port approaches.

Coastal charts are usually at scales of between 1:75,000 (about 1 mile to the inch) and 1:150,000.

Small-scale charts may be used for planning purposes, at scales down to about 1:3,500,000.

The smallest-scale British Government charts are 1:10,000,000 (about 140 miles to the inch), while the largest are 1:2,500 (about 70 yards to the inch).

Gnomonic Projection

One solution to the problem of representing polar areas is to use an alternative projection, often described as gnomonic.

Like Mercator's projection, this is really a mathematical concept, but it can easily be visualised as the image that would be produced by a translucent globe, with a bright light at its centre, standing on a flat sheet of paper. Of course, the globe could be touching the paper at any point, but for polar charts the obvious place to choose would be the pole itself. This point of contact is known as the tangent point – because the paper is tangential to the globe at that point.

On any gnomonic chart, the meridians appear as straight lines, while parallels of latitude appear as curves, but the overall pattern varies considerably depending on where the tangent point is located. If the tangent point is at the Equator, the meridians appear as straight parallel lines. If the tangent point is the Pole, the pattern is more like a spider's web, in which the meridians are straight lines radiating outwards from the Pole, with the parallels of latitude as a series of concentric circles.

Gnomonic projection is reasonably good at showing very small areas close to its tangent point, so it was once widely used for very large scale charts such as harbour plans. Unfortunately, as you move away from the tangent point it distorts distance, direction, shape and area to such an extent that it becomes almost useless for everything except one particular purpose.

Polar Charts

Nowadays, few charts of polar areas use the gnomonic projection.

Instead, to minimise the distortion of distance, they are drawn on a projection known as UPS (Universal Polar Stereographic). This is similar to gnomonic projection, in that meridians appear as straight lines and parallels as concentric circles, but the change of spacing between the parallels is reduced.

UPS can best be visualised as the image that would be cast by a translucent globe standing on a flat sheet of paper, but with the illumination provided by a bright light at the opposite pole, instead of at the centre.

The unique characteristic of gnomonic charts that has ensured their survival is that the gnomonic projection is the only one on which the shortest distance between two points (known as the great circle route) appears as a straight line. For planning ocean passages, particularly those with a large east-west movement, the distance saved can be significant.

Transverse Mercator Projection

Gnomonic projection stopped being used for harbour plans during the 1970s, when it was largely superseded by the transverse Mercator projection. In simple terms, this can be visualised as the image that would be cast by an illuminated globe onto a cylinder of paper wrapped around it from pole to pole – touching the globe along a meridian, rather than around the Equator (Figure 30).

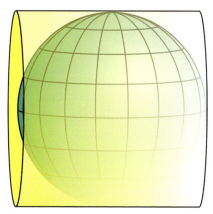

It distorts distances in much the same way as the conventional Mercator projection and shows both meridians and parallels as curved lines. It is, however, very good at portraying shape, and its distortions are negligible so long as you only look at a narrow band on each side of the central meridian. This makes it particularly useful for mapping long thin countries. It is the basis of all British Ordnance Survey maps, and – importantly for marine navigators – of the majority of large-scale charts such as harbour plans.

Figure 30

Charted Information

A navigational chart contains a huge amount of information. As well as the coastline, it also includes depths, represented by contour lines and spot soundings, heights, details of navigation aids such as lighthouses and buoys, hazards such as underwater pipelines and cables as well as rocks and sandbars, some rules and regulations such as traffic separation schemes, prohibited areas and forbidden anchorages, and supplementary information such as the type of seabed and facilities available ashore.

Surveys and Source Data

This information has not necessarily been collected from one source or at one particular time. On a chart of a British harbour, for instance, the offshore depth data may have come from two or three different naval survey ships at different times, while most of the land data comes from the Ordnance Survey – also based on several different surveys at different times. The harbour master may well have contributed a detailed survey carried out around a container berth, a marina operator may have provided details of the marina, and a fisherman may have added the position of an obstruction that snagged his nets. Electricity boards, telephone companies and such like will also have provided information about pipelines and cables.

On official charts, the main sources of information are listed in a source data diagram, like that shown in Figure 31. Charts from civilian publishers and Admiralty Leisure Folios seldom include as much information, but usually refer back to the Admiralty standard charts from which they are derived.

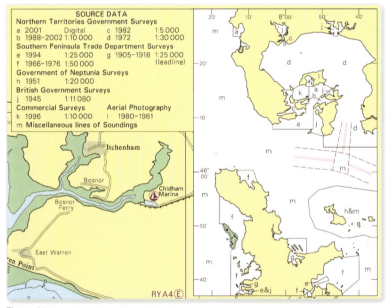

Figure 31

Where a source data panel is included, it is worth bearing in mind how survey techniques have changed over the years:

- Before 1935: Surveys were carried out using a lead and line. If the lead missed a rock by as little as a few inches it could go completely unnoticed. Until about 1900 many surveys (especially inshore) were carried out under sail or oars, so it was often not possible to take soundings in any well-defined pattern.
- 1935: The introduction of the echo sounder made continuous lines of sounding possible, but hazards between lines of sounding could be (and were) missed.
- 1973: Side-scan sonar was introduced. By 'looking sideways' as well as downwards, side-scan sonar made it possible to detect hazards lying between the lines of soundings.

There have been similar improvements in positioning accuracy over the same timescale, due to improved compasses in the late 19th century, radio navigation systems from 1945 onwards, and satellite navigation systems in the final quarter of the 20th century.

Many charts based on very old surveys are still in use, and hazards are still being discovered. Even a reasonably detailed modern survey could miss a rock the size of a super tanker if it happened to be midway between the lines of soundings and parallel to them.

Overall, the message is that charts based on old surveys need to be treated with caution.

Symbols and Abbreviations

A 200-metre chimney, standing out against the skyline and festooned with red lights at night, makes a magnificent landmark. Its base, however, may only be 25 metres in diameter, so even on a 1:25,000 chart it would be accurately represented by an inconspicuous spot just 1mm in diameter. On a typical coastal chart, it would appear as a barely visible speck. Important navigation marks such as buoys and beacons would be even smaller.

To overcome this kind of problem, cartographers (chart producers) use a myriad of symbols. The extract on pages 178–179 shows some of the most important ones used on British Admiralty charts: the definitive list of symbols and abbreviations is given in a booklet (called *Symbols and Abbreviations* used on *Admiralty Charts*, code 5011). Other chart publishers use different symbols, but they are generally sufficiently similar to the Admiralty ones that it's easy enough to switch between one chart and another, especially as – as a general rule and with a few notable exceptions such as churches – the symbol consists of a simple picture of the sort of thing it is meant to represent, with a small circle at its base to represent its actual position.

Electronic Chart Systems

One of the most exciting navigational developments of the past few years has been the introduction and rapid development of electronic charting systems, often called chart plotters. The big advantage of such things is that, when linked to an electronic position fixer such as GPS, they are able to show the boat's position, updated far more frequently than any human could hope to achieve, on an electronic representation of a chart. Their big drawbacks are that they are (perhaps arguably) less reliable and less intuitive than traditional paper and pencil.

Essentially, though, they do precisely the same three jobs as paper charts, pencils and drawing instruments. They are:

- A source of information.
- A means of carrying out calculations.
- A temporary record of navigational events.

Like almost any computer-based system, a chart plotter is made up of three distinct parts:

- Hardware – the physical equipment, including the screen, controls, computer etc.
- Data – the information the system uses, including the cartography (the electronic charts) and other data such as the boat's position, course, and speed.
- Software – the programme, or set of instructions which tell the hardware what to do with the data.

There are huge differences between the various chart plotting systems, but most fall into one of two groups which can conveniently be classified as 'hardware plotters' and 'PC-based' or 'software' plotters.

Hardware plotters are mainly produced by marine electronic specialists, and are designed and built specially for the job, with software included as an integral part of the package. They are generally rugged and waterproof, with customised control panels and reasonably user-friendly operating procedures, but their screens are often small – and large ones are very expensive.

Software plotters use computer software that is usually developed by relatively small, specialist companies to run on conventional desktop or laptop. Ruggedized and waterproofed hardware is available, but many people use a standard laptop with considerable success.

Non-ruggedized PCs are relatively cheap, particularly when compared with dedicated plotters with displays of similar size and when you bear in mind that the same PC can be used for many other jobs. Inevitably, though, there are concerns about the reliability of office equipment at sea, and about the back-up that is available to help users who experience difficulty when the system is made up of components bought from perhaps half a dozen different suppliers.

Electronic Charts

Despite the fact that most surveys now gather and collate information electronically, the end result is almost invariably converted into a paper chart. This, combined with the vast mass of data already available on paper charts dating back to the age of lead-line surveys (pre-1935), means that the starting point for the production of any electronic chart is likely to be its paper counterpart.

It is easy to forget, as you zoom in on a hi-tech, 21st-century plotter, that the basic information it shows can never be better than that on the paper charts from which it is derived, and which may have been gathered by lead and line swung from a ship that was beating to windward at the time!

The paper charts – or the individual colour separations that are used to print them – are scanned and converted into computer code. The process is similar to the way a fax machine scans a document and turns it into the crackle of pulses that you can hear when a fax machine

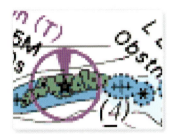

Figure 32

is connected to a telephone line. The big difference is that the computer code can be stored in any of several different types of electronic memory, which can then be read by the computer and reconstituted into an electronic replica of the original chart. It is not, however, a perfect copy, but is a raster image (Figure 32), made up of a mass of tiny rectangular blocks called picture elements or pixels. The result is that lines such as contours – which were smooth, continuous curves on the original – appear as strings of tiny squares on the reconstituted version.

For some electronic charts – including the Admiralty Raster Chart System (ARCS) – the process almost stops there. The result is an electronic chart that, when you see it on a computer screen, looks almost exactly like the paper chart from which it was derived. The only difference is that if you magnify it by using the zoom facility offered by most chart plotters, you can see the individual pixels.

That similarity to a paper chart – and the fact that they can be produced relatively quickly and cheaply – is the big advantage of raster charts.

One drawback of raster charts is that storing information about the position and colour of every tiny pixel that makes up a chart uses a huge amount of computer memory – on average about 1.5MB per chart, even after it has been electronically compressed.

In the early days of chart plotters – particularly hardware plotters – this was a big issue, so several commercial concerns adopted a more labour-intensive and time-consuming method, which involved tracing each chart and electronically processing the result into vector format.

Instead of breaking a line up into pixels, a coastline or contour on a vector chart is stored as a number of segments, rather like a child's join-the-dots picture (Figure 33). Instead of storing information about every pixel on the chart, vector systems only need to store the position of each bend in the line, and what kind of line it is supposed to represent. Objects too, such as buoys, can be saved as single chunks of data, rather than as clusters of pixels. Later versions are more refined, and slightly less frugal; they include more data about each line on the chart to indicate how much curvature it should have, for instance, but they still use a lot less memory.

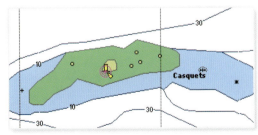

Figure 33

The vector format has also opened the way to the so-called intelligent chart system, which can (for instance) be set to trigger an alarm when the vessel approaches a shallow patch – something that would be impossible on a raster chart, where a contour line is simply a cluster of dots. A very common and very useful application of this kind of intelligence also makes it possible to reduce the number of charts that are needed by including all the information that is available on large-scale charts, but grouping it into 'layers'.

Raster v. Vector: the Official Line

Back in 1999, the International Maritime Organization published a comparison of raster and vector charting systems. It refers to official, type-approved systems for commercial shipping, but most of the comments apply equally to small craft.

ECDIS = Electronic Chart Display and Information System (vector)

RCDS = Raster Chart Display System (raster)

ENC = Electronic Navigational Chart (vector)

RNC = Raster Navigational Chart (raster)

GNSS = Global Navigational Satellite System

1. Unlike ECDIS where there are no chart boundaries, RCDS is a chart-based system similar to a portfolio of paper charts.

2. Raster Navigational Chart (RNC) data itself will not trigger automatic alarms (e.g. anti-grounding). However, some alarms can be generated by the RCDS from user-inserted information. These can include:

   • clearing lines • ship safety contour lines • isolated dangers • danger areas

3. Horizontal datums and chart projections may differ between RNCs. Mariners should understand how the chart horizontal datum relates to the datum of the position fixing system. In some instances this may appear as a shift in position. This difference may be most noticeable at grid intersections and during route monitoring.

4. Chart features cannot be simplified or removed to suit a particular navigational circumstance or task at hand. This could affect the superimposition of radar/ARPA.

5. Without selecting different scale charts the look-ahead capability may be somewhat limited. This may lead to some inconvenience when determining range and bearing or the identity of distant objects.

6. Orientation of the RCDS display to other than chart-up may affect the readability of chart text and symbols (e.g. course-up, route-up).

7. It may not be possible to interrogate RNC features to gain additional information about charted objects.

8. It is not possible to display a ship's safety contour or safety depth and highlight it on the RCDS display unless these features are manually entered during route planning.

9. Depending on the source of the RNC, different colours may be used to show similar chart information. There may also be differences in colours used during day and night time.

10. An RNC should be displayed at the scale of the paper chart. Excessive zooming in or zooming out can seriously degrade RCDS capability, for example, by degrading the legibility of the chart image.

11. Mariners should be aware that in confined waters the accuracy of chart data (i.e. paper charts, ENC or RNC data) may be less than that of the position-fixing system in use. This may be the case when using differential GNSS. ECDIS provides an indication in the ENC that allows a determination of the quality of the data.

As you zoom out to look at a larger area, the software can hide successive layers to remove clutter; as you zoom in, it can reinstate them to show more detail.

The price of computer memory may have been what drove electronic cartographers to choose vector format, but this kind of 'intelligence' has now made it very clearly the preferred choice. With effect from 2002, commercial ships (which are required under international law to carry 'adequate and up-to-date charts') can now use vector charts without paper back-ups. Raster charts are only accepted where vector chart coverage is inadequate, and must be backed up with paper ones.[4]

Electronic charts – Suppliers and Standards

There are very few 'dual fuel' chart plotters (i.e. able to use both raster and vector) available, though their numbers may increase over time.

At present, though, the dominant supplier of raster charts is the United Kingdom Hydrographic Office (UKHO), which publishes Admiralty paper charts and the Admiralty Raster Chart System (ARCS). The charts are supplied on CDs, each containing about 200 charts. When you buy a folio of 10 charts, however, you are supplied with a key-code which unlocks only the charts you have paid for. They are used mainly on PCs that have the memory and processor power required to decompress the data quickly, and relatively large screens.

The Admiralty is also developing an ENC service to supply vector charts known as S57 that conform to the specifications set by the International Maritime Organization (IMO).

Most of the commercial companies that produce electronic charts have concentrated on the vector format. Some produce S57 charts, but in general each company works to its own specifications, so a plotter designed to use C-Map NT+ charts, for instance, cannot use charts produced by Navionics or Transas.

The physical shape and size of the media in which the charts are supplied varies too. Some are supplied on CDs, either for use on PCs or so that the data can be downloaded through a PC into a hand-held unit, but most make use of some kind of memory 'chip' or 'card' – often an SD card identical to those used in digital cameras.

Keeping Charts Up-to-Date

On land, it may be frustrating to find yourself stuck in a traffic jam on a motorway that didn't exist when your road map was printed, or to find your plans thwarted by a no right turn that isn't shown on your street map.

---

[4] Under the International Safety of Life at Sea (SOLAS) Convention (revised 2000). In 2002, however, the British Government indicated that it would not accept vector charts as a substitute for paper charts on vessels in UK waters, because the UK Hydrographic Office (UKHO) had not produced enough of them to provide adequate coverage.

The same kind of thing at sea can have very much more serious consequences. It is far from unusual, for instance, for ships to be wrecked on the remains of earlier wrecks. To cope with shifting sandbanks, new wrecks, buoys that have been moved and new landmarks being built or old ones knocked down, charts need to be kept up-to-date.

The UKHO publishes new charts relatively rarely. More often an existing chart will be revised and updated and published as a new edition. This happens when there has been some major development, an extensive new survey, or a large number of minor changes. In some busy areas, new editions may be produced every few years. In others, one edition of a chart may last for 50 years or more.

To cope with more minor changes, it publishes Notices to Mariners on a weekly basis, making them available free of charge through its website www.ukho.gov.uk.

Before you start, though, it is worth sorting your charts into order and making a list of their numbers, with a note of the latest correction applied to each one. It should be shown in the bottom left-hand corner. Armed with that information, it's relatively easy to make sure that you download and either save or print all the relevant Notices to Mariners.

The Notices themselves can be divided into four main groups, of which by far the most common are 'pen and ink' corrections.

Pen and Ink Corrections

The first line of the Notice (Figure 34) contains the correction number, a description of the area concerned and a brief summary of the change.

> 3698* **ENGLAND, South Coast — The Solent and Isle of Wight — Ryde Middle and Ryde Pier Westwards — Beacon; Buoy; Fog signal**
>
> Substitute   port–hand beacon with topmark for port–hand can buoy   50° 44′·27N., 1° 09′·86W.
> Delete   fog signal, Bell, at S Ryde Middle light–buoy,
>   (chart 2045, fog signal, Bell, at starboard–hand
>   conical light–buoy)   (a)   50° 46′·13N., 1° 14′·15W.
>
> *Note:* **Positions** on both of the charts affected by this notice are referred to a **WGS84** compatible datum. See list of ADMIRALTY CHARTS OF GREAT BRITAIN THAT ARE REFERRED TO A WGS84 COMPATIBLE DATUM (near the beginning of this publication) and NM 4731(P)/00.
>
> **Chart** [*Last correction*].— **2036** (INT 1730) [2628/02] — **2045** (a) [3453/02]
> Queen's Harbour Master, Portsmouth   (*HH.232/600/08*).

Figure 34

The main body of the Notice tells you what to do: it is usually a straightforward instruction to 'Insert', 'Delete', 'Move', 'Amend' or 'Substitute', followed by a description of the object concerned and the position.

There is often a note stressing the horizontal datum concerned. If any of the charts effected by the change was drawn on the WGS84 datum or ETRS 89 then the positions given in the Notice will be based on the same datum. To plot them accurately on a chart that was drawn on one of the older datums (such as OSGB 36 or ED 50) you will have to apply a datum shift, following the instructions given on the chart itself under the heading 'Satellite-derived positions' (see page 11).

The last section of the Notice tells you which charts are affected by the it, which bits of the Notice apply to each chart, the number of the previous notice affecting that chart, and the source of the information.

It is worth looking at this small print because, in this particular example (Figure 34), for instance, it shows that only part (a) of the Notice applies to chart 2045, which could save you trying to find a position that isn't even on the chart! It also shows that the last correction affecting 2045 was number 3453/02 – so if the last correction to have been applied to it was something else, it shows that at least one has been missed.

In most cases, following the instruction is pretty simple. If you're told to 'insert' something, just draw in the appropriate symbol, with a little circle in the base of the symbol on the exact position. If you're told to 'delete' it, just cross it out. To 'move' something, you can either cross out the old one and draw a new one in its new position, or put a ring around the original one, with a curved arrow pointing to a small circle marking its new position. A similar approach will work for 'substitute' and 'amend', except that here you don't have to draw a new position circle.

The last stage of applying a correction is to write the number and the year in the bottom left-hand margin of the chart, so that when you next settle down to update your charts you don't find yourself skipping some corrections or trying to apply others twice.

Temporary and Preliminary Notices

Temporary and Preliminary Notices are very similar, except they relate to things that haven't happened yet or that are soon going to stop happening – such as major dredging works or regattas that involve temporary buoyage or exclusion zones. If possible, draw them onto the chart in just the same way as a normal correction, but in pencil.

Block Corrections

Block corrections are used when there is a particularly complicated change that is confined to a small part of a chart – such as the construction of a new marina (Figure 35). In this case, the Notice to Mariners is accompanied by a second file in Portable Document Format (PDF), which needs to be printed out in colour. A laser printer is best, because the results are waterproof, but most inkjet inks will do. By far the most important factor is that it must be printed at its original size, because the printed block is a patch that will be stuck over the out-of-date section of the original chart.

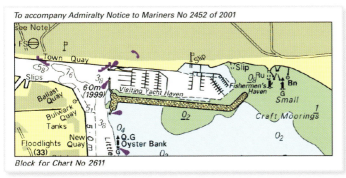

Block for Chart No 2611

Figure 35

Cut round it, just inside the border, and round off the corners slightly. The best glue to use is a 'lipstick'-type glue stick, because it's clean and easy to use, and lets you slide the block around for a few seconds, but then sticks quickly. Before you stick it down, though, have a dry run to make sure it really is the right size and that you know exactly where it is to go.

Leisure Folios and Civilian Charts

The Notices to Mariners system is aimed at users of the Admiralty's standard charts, but a very similar system applies to Leisure Folios, also available through www.ukho.gov.uk.

Commercial publishers have their own correction systems, but these are generally less frequent and comprehensive than the Admiralty's. Of course, the rocks, shoals, buoys and lighthouses mentioned in Notices to Mariners are not peculiar to Admiralty charts, so you can still use Notices to Mariners, but applying the information is trickier, because their numbering systems are different. One answer is to obtain an Admiralty chart catalogue, and use it to find out which Admiralty charts cover the area of your charts.

Correcting Electronic Charts

Electronic charts are no more immune from changes than paper ones, but the mechanisms for updating are different.

A part of the ARCS service is the provision of update disks. Unlike Notices to Mariners this is not a free service; the price depends on the number of charts you have and the frequency with which you want to update. The principle is very similar to block corrections on a paper chart, because the update disk contains a number of 'tiles', each of which is electronically 'cut' and 'pasted' onto the original charts to cover and replace a section that has been affected by a Notice to Mariners change.

The main commercial suppliers of vector charts for small craft have all adopted a 'service return' system, under which they offer an up-to-date replacement cartridge in exchange for an old one, at a fraction (typically 25–50 per cent) of the price of a new one.

Other Publications

Charts may be the main source of a navigator's information, but there are many other useful reference books. These include:

Tide Tables

Tide Tables (see page 89) predict the rise and fall of the tide at each of several 'standard ports'. Supplementary tables (difference tables) are usually included from which it is possible to work out very similar information for many smaller or less important 'secondary' ports.

Tidal Stream Atlases

Tidal Stream Atlases (see page 99) provide a graphic representation of the flow of the tidal streams in a particular area.

Lists of Lights

Lists of lights give more information about lighthouses and other lit navigational marks than could possibly be provided on a chart. At Polperro (2 miles east of Fowey, on the south coast of Cornwall), for instance, is a lighthouse that on the largest scale chart of the area is said to be

30m high – quite an impressive structure, you might think. The List of Lights, however, reveals that the light is exhibited from a white brick structure just 3m high. It isn't a magnificent tower at all, but something more like a garden shed perched halfway up a cliff.

Lists of Radio Signals

The Admiralty publishes seven volumes of lists of radio signals, some of which are divided into several separate books. Some, such as Volume 8 – Satellite Navigation Systems (there is no Volume 7!), are more like text books, while others list the positions, frequencies and services provided by radio stations, and associated rules and regulations.

Yachtsmen's Almanacs

Official Lists of Lights, Radio Signals, and tidal publications contain a lot of useful information but they are bulky, expensive and often not very user-friendly for small craft. Yachtsmen's almanacs, from various publishers, contain similar information but edited down (mainly by removing the 'big ship' stuff) to fit into a single book or loose-leaf folder. Most include other information, such as sunrise and sunset tables, and many include port information, simple harbour plans and lists of waypoints.

Yachtsmen's almanacs should not be confused with the Nautical Almanac, which gives astronomical data for astro-navigation and astronomers.

Pilots and Sailing Directions

Admiralty pilots and sailing directions are mainly aimed at ships. They provide a mass of detailed descriptive information that cannot be included in charts and draw attention to particular hazards, but they are bulky and not particularly user-friendly. Yachtsmen's pilots vary very widely in size, scope and style; some are essentially guide books for tourists, others are not unlike the Admiralty versions. Many include potted 'pilotage plans' for harbour entrances.

Summary
- A chart is a marine map drawn to scale. Large-scale charts cover small areas such as individual harbours, medium-scale charts are used for coastal navigation and small-scale charts cover large areas for planning purposes.
- Good-quality charts are updated regularly and show the source of the information on which they are based.
- Electronic charts can be displayed either on dedicated marine hardware (e.g. 'plotters' or 'MFDs') or on general-purpose computers.

6 POSITION FIXING

It would be nice to think that if you travel south-eastwards for 2 miles, you will end up 2 miles south-east of where you started. As in the example at the end of Chapter Four, that isn't necessarily the case:

- The helmsman may not be steering very accurately.
- There may be unknown log or compass errors.
- The wind may be pushing the boat sideways.
- The water itself may be moving due to ocean or river currents or tidal streams.

In real navigation, all four of these are likely to be happening at the same time, so fixing the boat's position – to find out where it really is as opposed to where you think it should be – is an important part of the navigational process.

A Single-Point Fix

One of the best possible fixes is sometimes called a single-point fix or a landmark fix, because it involves no more than passing close to a fixed and clearly identifiable landmark.

Ashore, we use this kind of position fix every day, often without thinking about it: "I'll meet you in the lounge bar of the Green Dragon," or "I'm just outside the chemist's in the High Street". Both involve landmark fixes.

At sea, the single-point fix is particularly useful at the start and end of a passage, when you are likely to be passing very close to either a harbour wall or to a pile or beacon marking a channel. Buoys can also provide easy single-point fixes, but they are not quite as good because they invariably move around by a few metres, and have been known to drag their anchors or disappear completely.

Nevertheless, in the example on page 45, passing close to the green buoy at the mouth of the Rampton Bay provides a perfectly reasonable fix at the start of a passage. It meets all the requirements for a single-point fix:

- It can be positively identified in the real world.
- Its position is clearly shown on the chart.
- It is possible to pass close enough to the landmark for the difference between our position and its position to be of no practical significance.

Position Lines

On land (Figure 36), a slightly more sophisticated kind of position fix is provided by the intersection of two line features. Line features include things such as streams, railways and overhead power cables, or any physical feature that can be represented as a line on a map or chart. Perhaps the simplest everyday example of an intersection fix is a cross-roads or motorway junction. You could, for instance, say "This service station is where the A-road crosses the motorway."

Figure 36

Suppose, for instance, you're driving southwards along the A-road. The mere fact that you know which road you are on tells you that your position must lie somewhere along the slightly wriggly green line that represents the A-road on your map. In more technical-sounding language, the A-road is a position line – a line on which your position lies.

As you pass across the motorway you are, for a moment, on two position lines at once: the motorway as well as the A-road.

Of course, there are no roads at sea, but there are plenty of other position lines available and plenty of uses to which they can be put.

Sources of position lines include:

- Astronomical (calculated from sextant sights of the sun or stars, and outside the scope of this book).
- Compass bearings (see page 130).
- Contour lines (see page 83).
- Ranges by dipping distance (see page 80).
- Ranges by radar (see page 170).
- Transits (see page 129).

Even satellite navigation systems, such as the Global Positioning System (GPS) depend on the principle of intersecting position lines.

The Global Positioning System (GPS)

The Global Positioning System isn't the world's first electronic position fixing system, nor is it the only one, and it certainly won't be the last. But at the moment (2013), this American satellite-based system is effectively in a monopoly position.

Development work on GPS started in 1973. At first, it was seen as a purely military system, to be designed and built for the American armed forces and their allies. It soon became apparent, however, that part of its capability could be made available to civilian users, and that doing so would make the enormous cost of this revolutionary system more acceptable to Congress and the US taxpayer.

The Background to GPS

The principle of GPS is simple and very much like the principle behind radar and even the echo sounder: if you know how long a signal takes to travel from one place to another, and you know how fast it is travelling, you can easily calculate the distance it has covered.

In the case of GPS, the transmitters are carried on board about two dozen satellites,[5] in orbits some 20,000 km above the Earth's surface. Each satellite carries several atomic clocks (all controlled by a ground station) and repeatedly broadcasts a coded message which says, "I am here, I am moving this way, and the time is now...".

Figure 37

It also broadcasts similar (but less accurate and less up-to-date) information about all the other satellites that make up the complete constellation.

By the time that message reaches a GPS receiver, somewhere on or near the surface of the Earth, time has moved on. By comparing the time at which the message was sent with the time at which it was received, and multiplying the difference by 300,000,000 (the speed of radio waves in metres per second) the receiver can calculate its distance from the satellite.

Suppose, for instance, that the signal arrives 0.07 seconds after it was sent. In 0.07 seconds a radio wave travels 21,000,000 metres, so the receiver must be somewhere on the surface of an invisible sphere, like a huge bubble in space, with the satellite at the centre and a radius of 21,000,000m. This sphere is a three-dimensional position line.

If the receiver then does the same thing with the signal from a second satellite it will produce a second bubble or position sphere, intersecting with the first one. In order to be on the surface of both spheres at once the receiver must be somewhere on the circle at which they intersect.

If it does the same with a third satellite it will narrow down the possible positions to two, of which one may well be highly improbable – well below ground level, perhaps, or a long way from the surface of the Earth. For an unambiguous fix, though, the GPS receiver needs the signal from at least one more satellite to produce a fourth position sphere, intersecting with the other three.

---

[5] The exact number of satellites varies slightly, as new satellites are launched and old ones break down. At the time of writing (September 2012) there are 31 satellites in the constellation.

Selective Availability

When GPS was first conceived, it was intended primarily as a very precise military system, whose receivers needed an approximate position (accurate to about 100 metres) in order to 'lock on' to the satellite signals. To achieve this, the satellites also transmitted a relatively simple signal known as the Coarse Acquisition Code. This CA Code is the only part of the signal that civilian GPS receivers are allowed to use.

As soon as the first few satellites became operational it was obvious that even the CA code was giving much better results than had been expected. To prevent civilian receivers being used for military purposes, the American Government adopted a policy of 'Selective Availability', under which deliberate errors were introduced to the CA code signal to degrade its accuracy to about 100 metres.

The policy was abandoned in May 2000. The US Government retains the ability to reintroduce it, but has declared that it has no intention of ever doing so.

Errors

In theory, at least, all four position spheres should intersect at a single point. In practice, they probably won't, because the range measurements on which each sphere is based are subject to a variety of errors. By far the biggest of these is receiver clock error.

Suppose the receiver clock is running just a thousandth of a second fast. It will over-state the time that each signal has been in flight by a thousandth of a second, so it will overstate the distance to each satellite by 300,000 metres, or about 162 nautical miles. Instead of intersecting at a single point, the position spheres will intersect to form a giant tetrahedron – a three-sided pyramid, hundreds of miles from top to bottom and from side to side.

When this happens, the computer within the GPS receiver recognises that there is a problem, and sets about adjusting its clock until the four position circles intersect as they should.

This removes the biggest single source of error, but it still leaves a number of smaller ones. These include:

- Atmospheric delays, caused by the satellite signal being bent as it passes through the atmosphere.
- Multipath errors, caused by the satellite signals reaching the receiver by some indirect route such as by being reflected from the surface of the sea. On land this can be a major problem, but at sea it can easily be minimised by keeping the antenna as low as possible.
- Satellite clock and position errors.
- Electronic noise, which makes it difficult for the receiver to detect the precise instant at which the timing pulses are received.

These errors all vary from moment to moment; they sometimes cancel each other out and at other times add together. Generally, though, they amount to a total range error in the order of about 10 metres on each satellite.

This does not, however, mean that GPS is accurate to 10 metres. The reason is a mathematical phenomenon known as dilution of precision (DOP). It is easiest to understand if you think of it in only two dimensions, rather than three. In Figures 38 and 39 the curving magenta line represents the position line obtained by measuring the range from one satellite, and the blue line represents the position line derived from another satellite. The corresponding tinted band surrounding each line represents the margin for error.

Where the two lines intersect at right angles (Figure 38), you'll see that the margins for error form a slightly distorted square shape, roughly 1.4 times as big, from corner to corner, as the original margin for error.

When the two position lines intersect at a shallower angle (Figure 39), the square-shaped area of uncertainty expands to form a diamond, which may be many times longer than the original range error.

Figure 38

At sea, with a well-positioned antenna and a full constellation of satellites, this 'dilution of precision' is seldom a problem. It only becomes significant when some of the satellites are masked by obstructions, such as may happen when a hand-held receiver is used in a boat's cabin, or when someone leans against an antenna mounted on a boat's pushpit.

On land, it is a common problem in urban canyons, where tall buildings block the signal from satellites on each side.

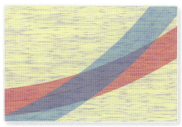

Figure 39

Accuracy

For all these reasons – varying errors and ever-changing values for the dilution of precision – if you were to sit at a fixed point and record a succession of GPS fixes, the result would be something like Figure 40, in which most of the fixes are pretty good, but there are a few that are much less impressive. If we had gone on recording fixes for long enough, there would undoubtedly have been some that were even worse.

To cope with this kind of thing, the accuracy of position-fixing systems is usually quoted at a particular 'level of confidence'. For marine navigation systems this is usually quoted at what mathematicians would describe as the 2drms or 2σ level. In practical terms, you can regard this as the radius of the circle which would include 95 per cent of all fixes. For most civilian GPS receivers it works out at about 15 metres.

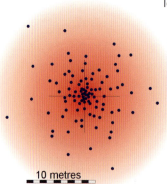

10 metres

Figure 40

Looking at the diagram, though, shows that it would be just as valid to quote an accuracy of 7 metres at 50 per cent level of confidence or 18 metres at the 99 per cent level.

Differential GPS

If you know about an error it can be corrected, just as a deviation card allows us to correct for deviation of a steering compass, and calibration allows us to correct the errors of a log.

The trouble with GPS errors is that they are unpredictable, so in order to correct them they have to be constantly monitored. It would be almost impossible to do that effectively on a moving platform such as a boat, but it can be done by using a fixed reference station to monitor the satellite signals. That is the principle behind differential GPS (dGPS).

Reference stations have been set up at fixed locations dotted around the world's coastlines. They monitor the satellite signals and compare the range measurements they obtain from each satellite with the figures they ought to be getting, and then broadcast the discrepancies by radio. To achieve worthwhile coverage from a ground-based transmitter calls for much lower frequencies than are used for GPS itself, and in practice most dGPS stations use the frequencies around 300kHz that were formerly used for radio direction finding. To receive such low frequencies requires a separate antenna and a special receiver, called a differential beacon receiver (DBR). The DBR then passes the information electronically to the GPS set, which – assuming it is described as differential ready – can apply the corrections to the satellite signals.

In the days of Selective Availability, this made a big difference to the accuracy that could be achieved, improving it from about 100 metres to about 8 metres. Now that Selective Availability has been switched off, and ordinary non-differential GPS is achieving accuracy in the order of 15 metres, the advantage is less obvious. However, dGPS still has a part to play in monitoring the integrity of GPS – giving a warning if, for any reason, the overall accuracy or reliability of the system starts to deteriorate.

The next stage in the development of GPS is already available. It is called satellite differential GPS (sdGPS), or by one of its regional acronyms, such as WAAS and EGNOS.

The American Wide Area Augmentation System (WAAS) covers the American continents, most of the Atlantic and the Eastern Pacific. It uses a network of reference stations, mostly in the USA, to monitor the signals received from the GPS satellites. The data is then collated, any spurious results rejected, and the consensus is passed up to several communication satellites that broadcast it to anyone with a suitable receiver. The accuracy achieved by WAAS is even better than terrestrial dGPS, but the really big advantage for small craft is that, because the correction signals are broadcast on the same frequencies as GPS signals, it does not require specialised receiving equipment, so the ability to receive and apply sdGPS corrections is being built in to many relatively modest GPS receivers.

The European Geostationary Navigational Overlay System (EGNOS) is very similar to WAAS, but covers the Eastern Atlantic and Europe, including the Baltic and Mediterranean.

Other Satellite Systems

Glonass

The former USSR began developing its Global Navigation Satellite System at about the same time as the USA started work on GPS, and launched its first satellite in 1982. In principle it was broadly similar to GPS, but Glonass was plagued by reliability problems: its satellites survived, on average, for fewer than three years, so it only briefly achieved a full constellation. The Russian Federation, however, has persevered with it and now (2013) has a full constellation of 24 operational satellites and five in-orbit spares. Its accuracy is comparable with GPS, and a growing number of civilian 'GPS' receivers are using Glonass signals as well as GPS.

Galileo

Galileo is the European counterpart of GPS. In principle it is broadly similar to GPS, but benefits from being a much more up-to-date system. Despite promises that it would have a constellation of 30 satellites and be fully functional by 2008, its first operational satellite was not launched until 2011.

It seems likely that Initial Operational Capability will be achieved in the next few years. Full operational capability is scheduled for "the end of the decade", and should provide positioning accuracy to about 5m, and a range of other services including a distress alerting system.

Beidou

China is developing its own satellite system called Beidou. Using completely different principles to GPS, Glonass or Galileo, it launched its first satellite in 2000, and achieved a limited operational capability with four satellites in 2007. A second, improved system has been introduced, and a third is being rolled out, both of which intend to give worldwide coverage by 2020.

Using GPS

GPS receivers are readily available in a wide variety of shapes, sizes and prices, including hand-held models priced at about £100, black box versions that have no display or controls of their own but are intended to provide basic time and position data to a computer or to other instruments, and bulkhead-mounted units with remote antennas that can be mounted on a boat's cabin roof or pushpit. Operating procedures vary almost as much as the range of designs.

• Do not be afraid to read the instructions.

All GPS sets, however, require time to search for satellites and lock on. If the unit has been stored without batteries or has been moved while switched off, this may take as much as 20 minutes, because it has to find one satellite and then wait to download details of all the others before it can start to calculate its first fix.

This cold-start process can be reduced to 2 minutes or so if the set is able to carry out a warm start, in which it already has some information about the constellation in its memory and it knows roughly where it is. It is very helpful if you can tell it the date, time and give it a position accurate to within a hundred miles or so.

Most sets include a satellite status display, which will show you how it is getting on with the process. It may also show you which satellites the receiver is using and warn you of any that it expects to be receiving but can't – perhaps because they are obscured.

While the GPS receiver is searching for satellites, it is a good opportunity for you, the user, to make sure that it is set to the right datum (see page 9) and that it is using the right position format and units for your purposes. At sea, you are likely to want position expressed as latitude and longitude rather than as Ordnance Survey grid references, for instance, and will probably prefer nautical miles to kilometres.

As soon as the receiver has calculated its position it is likely to switch automatically from the satellite status screen to a position display, showing its position and the direction and rate of movement. It is important to appreciate that a GPS receiver is not a compass, nor a log:

it shows the direction you are moving, not the direction the boat is pointing, and it shows your speed over the ground, not your speed through the water (Figure 41). If you are not moving, the direction indicated will be entirely random and may fluctuate wildly, but it will become much more stable as your speed increases.

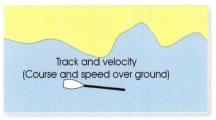

Figure 41

Waypoint Functions

Almost all GPS sets have a facility to store positions that are of special interest, known as waypoints (sometimes called route points or landmarks).

Once the unit's memory has stored a waypoint, and it has been told that you want to go to that waypoint (often by pressing a button marked Go To), it will then show the direction and distance you need to travel (Figure 42). While you are en route to the waypoint it will also show how far you have strayed from the straight line route – known as your cross-track error or XTE – and may give an estimated time of arrival or time to go, based on your present speed (Figure 43).

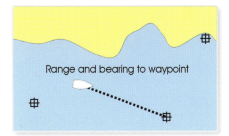

Figure 42

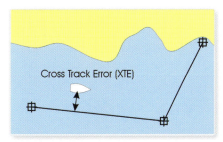

Figure 43

Plotting GPS Positions

Knowing your position, no matter how accurately, is of very limited value unless you can relate it to the world around you – to your starting point and destination, to any hazards that may be nearby and to any helpful features such as shelter or a favourable tidal stream. To do so, the position indicated by a GPS set has to be plotted on a chart.

Latitude and Longitude

The most obvious way to plot a GPS position is to use the latitude and longitude shown on the position display. Exactly how you do this depends to some extent on the plotting instruments you have available or have chosen to use, but the general idea is to use a pencil to draw a short section of the relevant meridian and parallel.

Suppose, for instance, that the GPS indicates a position of 50° 35'.7N 005° 48'.4W.

Using parallel rulers or plotters, the first step would be to line up the rulers with the nearest printed parallel of latitude and then open them up until one edge passes through 50° 35'.7N on the latitude scale, in order to draw a short section of this particular parallel on the chart (Figure 44).

Next, find a convenient meridian and use dividers to measure along the longitude scale to the 005° 48'.4W. Transfer the dividers to the pencilled parallel of latitude and with one point on the printed meridian make a pencil mark alongside the other point (Figure 45).

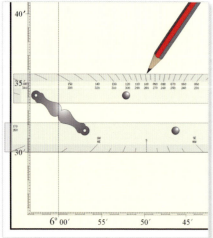

Figure 44

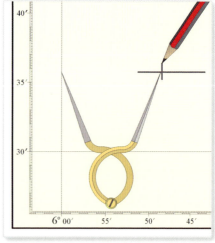

Figure 45

It's not essential to do things in this order: in some instances it may be easier to use the parallel rulers to draw a meridian and use dividers to measure latitude; in others it may be easier to use the parallel rulers for both co-ordinates.

No matter how you do it, though, plotting a latitude and longitude like this can easily take a couple of minutes – time which might be better spent on something else.

Quick Plotting Techniques

By Range and Bearing

Waypoints were originally conceived as points that you wanted to pass through on your way to somewhere, but the fact that GPS sets are able to give ranges, bearings and cross-track errors virtually instantaneously opens up other ways of plotting position.

Suppose, for instance, that the navigator on *Proud Maiden's* short passage from Quarry Marina to Endal (see page 45) had entered the position of the buoy off Webb Ellis Island as a waypoint,[6] and at 1730hrs had noticed that the GPS was showing its range and bearing as 2.9 miles, 320°(T).

If the bearing of the buoy from *Proud Maiden* is 320°(T), then the bearing of *Proud Maiden* from the buoy must be the reciprocal (opposite). To calculate a reciprocal, either add or subtract 180° (whichever produces a sensible answer).

In this case it is 320° - 180° = 140°(T).

In other words, *Proud Maiden's* 1730hrs position lies somewhere along a line drawn in a 140°(T) direction from the buoy (Figure 46).

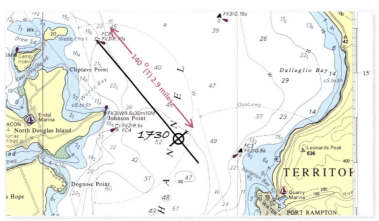

Figure 46

This, by itself, is of little use: she could be anywhere between Webb Ellis Island and Port Rampton. However, the fact that she is also 2.9 miles from the buoy narrows it down considerably because, by measuring a distance of 2.9 miles along the line from the buoy, it is possible to plot a position that is almost as accurate as by using latitude and longitude, but much more quickly and with less chance of making a mistake.

---

[6] In practice, it is best NOT to use objects such as buoys as target waypoints, because the accuracy of GPS is such that there is a very real risk of hitting your target! It is better to put the waypoint near the target rather than right on it.

Variations on Range and Bearing

Of course, there is no reason why the range and bearing technique has to use the waypoint you are aiming for. It may be the most obvious choice, but it is not necessarily the best. In general terms, it is best to base any kind of fix on near objects rather than distant ones, so at the start of a passage it is better to refer back to the waypoint you have just left, rather than to the one that is in front but further away.

Another possibility is to use a purely arbitrary waypoint, such as the centre of one of the compass roses printed on the chart (Figure 47). The beauty of this is that it makes it very easy to plot the bearing accurately: you don't even need parallel rulers or a plotter – any straight edge will do, because it can be lined up directly on the compass rose itself.

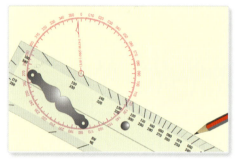

Figure 47

A variation on this idea is to draw your own compass rose around a waypoint that you are likely to use regularly, such as the entrance to your home port, and add range rings – concentric circles, drawn at regular intervals – to produce a pattern rather like a spider's web (Figure 48). This technique requires forward planning as it takes time to construct the spider's web, but it is particularly useful for very small or very fast boats because it means that a position can be plotted quickly when you are under way, without any chartwork instruments whatsoever.

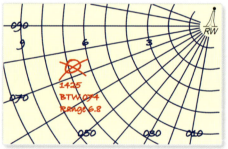

Figure 48

Range and Cross-Track Error

One of the problems associated with any position fix that involves using a bearing (direction) is that the positioning error associated with any error in the bearing becomes very large at long ranges. In the case of Figure 46, for instance, where the buoy was 2.8 miles away, a couple of degrees' error in drawing the line representing the bearing would have produced a position error of about 170 metres. Had we been dealing with a lighthouse 28 miles away, the positioning error would have been ten times as large – nearly a mile.

One way to deal with this is to use the GPS set's cross-track error (XTE) function rather than the bearing to waypoint.

On most longish passages, a part of the planning process is likely to involve marking your intended route onto the chart, with a waypoint at each bend. With this information already on the chart when you set out, monitoring your position by range and XTE is quick and simple.

Suppose, for instance, that *Princess Ida* is 4.8 miles from her next waypoint. It is easy for her navigator to measure back from the waypoint along the line showing the planned route and to make a mark 4.8 miles from the waypoint.

If, at the same time, the cross-track error display shows that she is 0.7 miles to starboard of her planned track, it is very nearly as easy for him to measure 0.7 from the mark he's just made, at right angles to the intended track, and label that as his position.

With a little more effort in the planning stage this technique can be made even easier by drawing lines parallel to the intended track, but a mile or half a mile on each side of it, and by marking up the distance to go to the waypoint, as in Figure 49.

This ladder or railway line plot has a lot in common with the spider's web that is used for plotting range and bearing and is particularly useful for the same types of

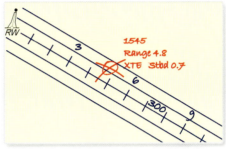

Figure 49

boats with limited navigation facilities, or lively motion, or single-handers. Its drawback is that speed and simplicity is achieved only at the expense of some accuracy. So long as the cross-track error is relatively small compared with the distance to the waypoint, the positioning error is unlikely to be significant.[7]

Chart Plotters

Perhaps the ultimate in quick plotting techniques is provided by an electronic plotter. Like so many pieces of marine equipment, chart plotters come in a vast range of sizes, prices and types, but what they all have in common is that they present a continuously updated graphic representation of the boat's present position, on a screen showing an electronic chart of the world around it.

In most cases, once the plotter has been switched on and supplied with position information (often from a GPS receiver, built into the plotter itself) and chart information from some form of electronic memory, this most basic function of a plotter is carried out entirely automatically.

---

[7] If the cross-track error is 20 per cent of the range, positioning error (in theory) is 2 per cent of the range or 10 per cent of the cross-track error, e.g.:

If Range = 5 miles and XTE = 1 mile, position error = 185 metres.

At long ranges, the performance of the ladder plot improves, e.g.:

If Range = 60 miles and XTE = 1 mile, positioning error = 15 metres.

Other Means of Fixing Position

GPS didn't exist until a quarter of a century ago. It was preceded by several land-based radio navigation systems including Decca, Loran and RDF. Decca and LDF are obsolete, and although the Loran system is being modernised, it has had little impact on leisure craft.

More traditional methods of navigating and fixing position, however, are still alive and well, serving as ideal complements and back-ups to GPS as well as forming a 'stand-alone system' in their own right.

The Three-Point Fix

For generations of seafarers, the three-point fix has been the cornerstone of coastal navigation. Unlike the single-point fix (see page 62) it does not involve passing close to a fixed object; it is quite possible to obtain a three-point fix 20 miles or more from the nearest landmark by using intersecting position lines.

There are several possible sources of position lines, but the most common are visual bearings taken by using a hand-bearing compass to measure the direction of your line of sight from the boat to a landmark such as a headland or a conspicuous building.

Hand-Bearing Compasses

Hand-bearing compasses can be divided into two main groups: arm's length and close-up versions. Both are essentially small versions of a boat's magnetic steering compass, consisting of a compass card and carrying several magnetic needles or a circular ring magnet that is free to pivot in a fluid-filled bowl. Unlike a steering compass, though, a hand-bearing compass has some form of sighting arrangement that allows the user to look at a distant object and at the compass card at the same time.

Some have an arrangement of prisms or mirrors to make an image of the compass card appear to float in mid-air above distant objects, others use simple pointers and notches as sights on top of an edge-reading compass card. Some are built into binoculars, and a few use flux gate technology (see pages 15–16) instead of a swinging card. Which is best is very much a matter of personal preference, though spectacle wearers generally find that they get on marginally better with the arm's length types.

Taking and Plotting a Fix

Taking a visual three-point fix involves measuring the direction of your line of sight to each of three objects in turn.

Suppose, for instance, that the yacht *Nekaya* is somewhere off Colville (Figure 50) and her skipper takes a bearing of the left-hand (southern) edge of the conspicuous Morgan Island: it's 289°(C).

Variation in this area is 7°W, and deviation, on a hand-bearing compass, must be assumed to be nil (see page 21), so the True bearing of Morgan Island is 289° - 7° = 282°(T). What this

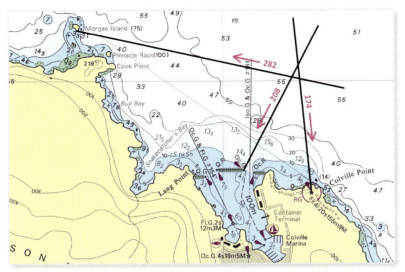

Figure 50

means is that the skipper's line of sight could be represented on the chart by a line drawn in a 282° direction, which just brushes the southern tip of the rock.

As with the range and bearing plot of a GPS position on pages 70 and 71, this isn't really much use on its own: *Nekaya* could be almost anywhere between Morgan Island and Colville Point.

Immediately after taking the bearing of Morgan Island, however, *Nekaya's* skipper also took a bearing of the eastern end of Colville breakwater. Making the same correction for variation, this yielded a True bearing of 208°(T). Using exactly the same logic as for the Morgan Island line, the implication of this is that *Nekaya* must be somewhere on the line drawn in a 208° direction that passes through the end of the breakwater.

There is only one place where she can possibly be on both lines at once – and that is where they intersect. Two intersecting position lines, in principle, are enough for a fix, but there must always be an element of uncertainty about the accuracy and reliability of a two-point fix. It would be too easy to take bearings of the wrong landmark, or to have added variation instead of subtracting it, or simply to have misread the compass. Two lines will usually intersect somewhere, without necessarily being right, and without any indication that there is something wrong, so it is always best to take a third bearing. Each line then serves to check the other two.

In this case, *Nekaya's* skipper took a bearing of the mighty lighthouse on Colville Point, converted it to True, and came up with an answer of 174°.

In theory, one might expect all three lines to cross at a single point. In practice, however, they rarely do. Just like the position spheres of GPS (see page 64) they miss each other, though in this case they form a two-dimensional triangle called a cocked hat, rather than a three-dimensional tetrahedron.

Unlike a GPS fix, in which it is a fair bet that receiver clock error accounts for most of any errors, we can't usually justify 'fudging' a visual fix by adjusting the bearings. There are simply too many possible sources of error, ranging from unknown deviation to the simple fact that the boat has moved while the bearings were being taken, so it wasn't actually in the same place when the third bearing was taken. It is better to plot the bearings as accurately and honestly as possible, and accept that they are unlikely to produce a pinpoint fix.

The size of the cocked hat is, itself, a crude indicator of the reliability of the fix. A neat, compact triangle generally – though not invariably – implies a much more reliable fix than an ungainly one that straggles around all over the chart.

There are a number of things one can do to keep the size of the cocked hat to a minimum and to make sure that the fix is as reliable and accurate as possible, summed up by six rules:

- Use landmarks that can be positively identified on the chart, as well as in the real world.
- Take bearings as accurately as possible.
- Take bearings as quickly as possible.
- Choose objects that are well spread around the horizon – ideally either 60° or 120° apart.
- Choose near objects rather than distant ones.
- Take bearings which are changing slowly first, and ones which are changing quickly last.

One would not normally write the bearings alongside the lines that represent them. Whilst it is classic navigation practice to keep a record of the bearings in a navigator's notebook or in the boat's deck log, writing them on the chart is only likely to cause confusion. Nor is it necessary to draw the full length of each position line. Instead, it is better to draw only the relevant part of each position line and to rub out any excess.

The Circular Fix

One particular case in which the size of the cocked hat can be particularly misleading is where the landmarks and your position all lie on or near the circumference of the same circle, and where all the bearings are wrong by about the same amount, such as might be caused by deviation. In these circumstances, a small cocked hat may be produced even if the fix is very wrong.

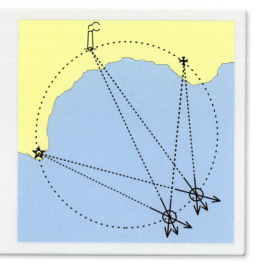

Mark the end of the remaining section with an arrowhead pointing away from the landmark –
the standard chartwork symbol for a visual bearing – and finish off the fix by drawing a circle
around the intersection and labelling it with the time at which it was taken and the log reading
(Figure 51).

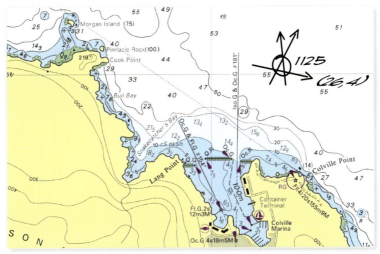

Figure 51

The Six Rules:

(1) Identification

Almost any charted object can serve as a landmark for fixing, but the best are compact but
conspicuous, such as lighthouses, churches and chimneys, or natural landmarks such as
pointed rocks or steep-sided headlands (Figure 52). It almost goes without saying, though, that
there is no point taking a bearing of something if you can't identify it on the chart as well as in
the real world. Many coastal towns, for instance, have several churches, but they are all useless
for fixing unless you can identify which is which.

Other features may seem conspicuous on the
chart but can be very difficult to pinpoint in the
real world. A spot height, marking the summit of
a hill, is a good example. Even more tempting
but even more misleading is a sloping headland
(Figure 53), whose edge seems clearly defined
on the chart, but which seems, when seen from
a boat, to merge almost imperceptibly with
the sea. At Low Water especially it can be very
difficult to be certain where the foreshore ends
and the charted coastline begins, while at long
distances it is quite possible for the tip of a low-
lying headland to be invisible below the horizon.

Figure 52

Figure 53

(2) and (3) Accuracy v. Speed

If a compass needle really pointed resolutely northward, taking an accurate bearing would be easy. Unfortunately, it doesn't. Quite apart from the unknown and unknowable error of deviation, there is also the inconvenient fact that any real compass card and needle weigh something, and are supported on a less than perfect pivot in less than perfect fluid. The upshot is that, unless the boat is perfectly still, the compass card is bound to swing somewhat erratically from side to side.

In general, the best results are obtained by lining up the compass with the object, holding it as steady as possible for a few seconds while the card settles itself from a few big swings of maybe 100° or more to a more manageable swing of perhaps 5° or 10° each way, before carrying out a mental average of a succession of small swings. Inevitably, though, this takes time – especially if you are trying to be particularly accurate – during which the boat is still moving. If you spend a minute on each bearing, then even at 6 knots the boat will have moved over a quarter of a mile in the time it takes to take one fix.

Speed and accuracy both improve with practice, but it is still, ultimately, impossible to combine the two. As a simple rule, for objects at short ranges speed is more important than precision, but for distant objects the priorities are reversed.

(4) Spread

When plotting a visual bearing the thin pencil line that represents each bearing looks reassuringly precise. In practice, though, it is impossible to use a hand-bearing compass with anything like the same degree of precision. In calm conditions it is often possible to take a bearing accurate to within 2°, but when the going gets rough it may be difficult to get within 10°.

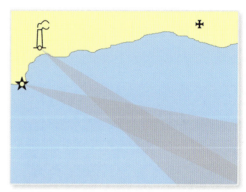

Figure 54

A more realistic way of representing each bearing – if only it were easier to draw on the chart – would be a fan-shaped beam, with fuzzy edges. The effect is shown in Figure 54, showing that where the angle between two landmarks is small, the intersection of the two fan-shaped beams produces a long, roughly diamond-shaped area of uncertainty.

As the angle between the two objects increases, the size of the area of uncertainty reduces until – at an angle of intersection of 90° – it becomes roughly square (Figure 55).

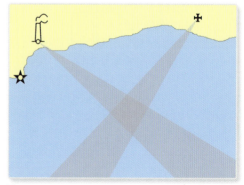

Figure 55

Compare this with the dilution of precision, which affects GPS fixes (page 66).

For three objects the same principle applies, except that the optimum angle between landmarks is either 60° or 120° (Figure 56).

It is always worth being particularly careful to avoid taking bearings of objects that are nearly 180° apart; the position lines they produce will be in opposite directions but almost parallel, and in many cases may not meet at all!

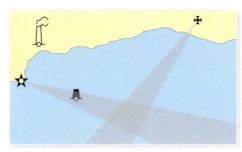

Figure 56

(5) Distance

If you try taking a bearing of an object at very short range, such as a buoy 100 metres away (Figure 57) it is almost impossible to get an accurate result, because the bearing is changing so quickly. This makes it tempting to choose more distant objects whose slowly-changing bearing makes it much easier to get a precise measurement.

Figure 57

This almost intuitive decision is the wrong one, however, because it ignores the fact that the bearing is only a means to an end: it is our position rather than the bearing that is of most interest. So the ideal situation is one in which a small change in position produces a noticeable change of bearing. After all, if the bearing changes 10° when the boat has only moved 15 metres (as it would if we were passing 100m from the buoy) it suggests that a measurement error of 10° would only produce a positioning error of about 15m. If, on the other hand, the bearing were of a lighthouse 15 miles away, the same bearing error would produce a position line that is wrong by some 2.5 miles!

(6) Fastest Last

If you are steering straight towards something, or directly away from it, its bearing changes only slowly, if at all. Therefore, when you take the bearing makes very little difference to the position line that you eventually draw on the chart.

The bearings of objects alongside you, by contrast, are likely to change quickly as you go past them, so the bearing becomes out-of-date very quickly.

To make sure you have the freshest fix possible, take the slow-changing bearing first and the fast-changing one last.

Other Sources of Position Lines

There are several other sources of position lines available to the navigator who chooses to use traditional methods.

Transit

One of the most useful, because it is quick, easy and can be uncannily accurate, is known as a transit. The formal definition of a transit is 'two objects on the same bearing from an observer'. In more everyday language, this means that a transit occurs when you see one object pass in front of another.

At that particular moment, when you and the two objects are all in line with each other, you can draw a position line on the chart without any instruments other than a straight edge with which to draw a line passing through both objects.

Because it uses no instruments, and is therefore immune from variation, deviation and most human errors, a transit is generally very accurate.

This combination of speed, precision and simplicity makes transits so useful that they are often set up deliberately, with posts, towers or lights carefully positioned to indicate a particular line – such as the safe channel into a harbour, a yacht race starting line, or the start and end of a measured distance.

These man-made transits are often shown on charts or mentioned in pilot books, along with particularly useful naturally occurring transits, but transits don't have to have such official 'approval' before they can be used: any two objects will do, so long as they are clearly identifiable on the chart as well as in the real world, and are reasonably far apart (as in Figure 58). What constitutes 'reasonable' depends mainly on how sensitive you need the transit to be.

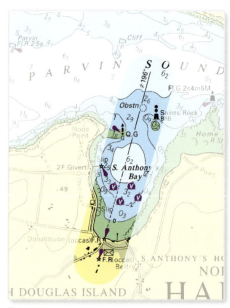

Figure 58

Range Measurement

Although compass bearings and transits between them probably account for the majority of fixes taken by traditional methods, there are occasions when range-based position lines are useful. A common example is when you are well offshore and heading directly towards or away from the coast, so that the only visible landmarks are clumped in a narrow arc ahead or astern. Position lines based on bearings become unreliable because they intersect at narrow angles, so range-based position lines become much more useful.

Measuring range – your distance from an object – is unfortunately difficult, and in most cases calls for specialist equipment such as a sextant, a rangefinder or radar. One method, however, requires no specialist equipment at all.

It relies on the fact that the Earth is round, so as you sail away from something it disappears below the horizon. Unfortunately, in most cases it is very difficult to tell the exact moment at which something disappears, and even more difficult to tell when it first appears.

The exception is a lighthouse, because at night, as you head towards it, the first thing you are likely to see is the 'loom' of the light, sweeping across the sky like a searchlight. As you get closer, the loom intensifies, and the individual rays seem to shorten until – quite suddenly – the light itself appears above the horizon as a much brighter and very distinct pinprick of light.

Am I Inside the Cocked Hat?

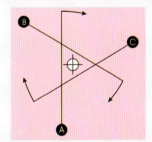

The answer is 'probably not'. There is (at least in theory) only a 25 per cent chance of your being inside the cocked hat.

Assume you know your position by some other means, but nevertheless are about to take a three-point fix on three landmarks, 120 degrees apart.

The first position line (on landmark A) is infinitely narrow, so the chances of it passing through your exact position are infinitesimal: your position, in other words, must lie to the right of it or to the left. In the diagram, our position is to the right of it.

This means that, in order to create a cocked hat that surrounds our position, the other position lines must pass us so as to leave us on the right-hand side of both of them.

If our position had been to the left of the first position line, the whole diagram would have been mirror-imaged, and the other lines would have had to pass us on their left as well.

The chance of the second line passing the correct side of us is only 50 per cent. In the 50 per cent of fixes that achieve this, the chance of the third line also passing on the correct side is also only 50 per cent. So the chance of all three lines passing us on the same side as the first one is:

$$100 \text{ per cent} \times 50 \text{ per cent} \times 50 \text{ per cent} = 25 \text{ per cent}$$

Canny navigators take account of this and seldom assume that they are in the centre of the cocked hat. It is better to assume that you are in the worst corner of the cocked hat – the one closest to danger – and to bear in mind that even that might be unduly optimistic!

The distance at which this happens is known as the dipping distance or rising distance, and depends on the height of the light and on your height of eye above the waterline.

It stems from the fact that the distance to your horizon depends mainly on the height of your eye above sea level, according to the formula:[8]

$$\text{Range (miles)} = 2 \times \sqrt{\text{Height (metres)}}$$

If you imagine a lighthouse keeper standing with his eyes level with his light and looking out to sea at the same time as you are looking shoreward from the sea, you will initially be out of sight of each other, hidden by the curvature of the Earth. As you make progress towards the land, however, your horizon will edge closer to the lighthouse keeper's horizon until they touch. At that moment, given a powerful enough pair of binoculars, you could, at least in theory, see each other above your shared horizon.

So the rising or dipping distance of a light can be worked out from the formula:

$$\text{Range (miles)} = (2 \times \sqrt{\text{Height (eye)}}) + (2 \times \sqrt{\text{Height (light)}})$$

Suppose, for instance, that your height of eye above water level is 2m, and the lighthouse has a charted elevation (height) of 36m. Strictly speaking, the elevation needs to be adjusted to allow for the actual height of tide below MHWS (see page 42) but, except for very low tides or very short lighthouses, the effect of the extra calculation is negligible.

$$\text{Range (miles)} = (2 \times \sqrt{\text{Height (eye)}}) + (2 \times \sqrt{\text{Height (light)}})$$

becomes:

$$\text{Range (miles)} = (2 \times \sqrt{2}) + (2 \times \sqrt{36}) = (2 \times 1.4) + (2 \times 6) = 2.8 + 12 = 14.8$$

---

[8] In theory, the multiplication factor should be 1.92 rather than 2, but in practice the distance to the horizon is slightly extended by atmospheric refraction, so 2 is a good approximation.

Rising and dipping distance tables, like the one in Figure 59, are included in the Admiralty List of Lights, most yachtsmen's almanacs, and various other reference books.[9]

Lights – distance off when rising or dipping (M)

Height of light			1	2	3	4	Height of eye 5
metres	feet	metres feet	3	7	10	13	16
10	33		8·7	9·5	10·2	10·8	11·3
12	39		9·3	10·1	10·8	11·4	11·9
14	46		9·9	10·7	11·4	12·0	12·5
16	53		10·4	11·2	11·9	12·5	13·0
18	59		10·9	11·7	12·4	13·0	13·5
20	66		11·4	12·2	12·9	13·5	14·0
22	72		11·9	12·7	13·4	14·0	14·5
24	79		12·3	13·1	13·8	14·4	14·9
26	85		12·7	13·5	14·2	14·8	15·3
28	92		13·1	13·9	14·6	15·2	15·7
30	98		13·5	14·3	15·0	15·6	16·1
32	105		13·9	14·7	15·4	16·0	16·5
34	112		14·2	15·0	15·7	16·3	16·8
36	118		14·6	15·4	16·1	16·7	17·2
38	125		14·9	15·7	16·4	17·0	17·5

Figure 59

Plotting a Range-Based Fix

If you know that a lighthouse is 14.8 miles from you, then you must also be 14.8 miles from it. In other words, you are somewhere on the circumference of a circle whose centre is at the lighthouse and whose radius is 14.8 miles. To plot the position line the ideal tool is a pair of drawing compasses with which to draw a short section of the relevant circle.

Of course, a single range, by itself, produces only one position line. It is very tempting to cross it with a bearing of the same object to produce a perfect-looking fix made up of two position lines that cut at right angles (Figure 60). This is perfectly acceptable if you are only after an approximate position and you are aware that the whole fix depends on the correct identification of a single lighthouse that you are seeing at the very limit of its visible range.

Figure 60

Contours

Contours can also serve as position lines (Figure 61). The logic is that if, having corrected your echo sounder reading for the height of tide, you find that you are in a depth of 50m, then you must be somewhere on a 50m contour line. Of course, the chances

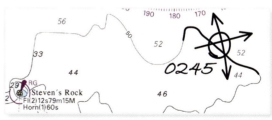

Figure 61

of your just happening to be on a contour line at the moment you choose to take a fix are very slim; more often you will have to consider the height of tide (see page 39) and then watch the echo sounder as it shallows or deepens towards a likely contour.

[9] Tables are usually based on multiplication factors ranging from 2.03 (Admiralty) to 2.095.

Mixed Fixes

Contour lines, by definition, can never cross, and you would have to be remarkably lucky to find yourself on two transits simultaneously, so either of these two important types of position line are normally used in combination with other position lines to make up what is sometimes called a mixed fix.

There is really nothing special about a mixed fix because there is no rule that says that just because you used a visual bearing for one line you must use visual bearings for the other two. The most important considerations are whether the position lines intersect at a suitable angle and whether they are sufficiently accurate.

Traditional Navigation and Chart Plotters

Chart plotters – especially dedicated hardware plotters, as opposed to PC-based software plotters – appear to pose something of a problem, in that it is difficult to draw lines on their screens and that it therefore seems difficult to use traditional methods to cross-check the position.

The problem disappears, however, if you remember that the main object of using traditional methods in this situation is to provide a cross-check, rather than a complete duplication of the work that the electronics have already done.

You can, in other words, make use of a single position line whenever one presents itself rather than having to look for them in groups of three at a time.

In the situation shown in Figure 62, for instance, the plotter is displaying our current position as a black circle (A) with our past track as a solid black line behind it and our predicted track as a dotted line ahead of it. Our Course over Ground is 053°. In this situation, it is quite likely that the navigator might have checked his position by looking at the transit (B) as he went past it. Now, approaching the shallows (C) – and with a number of broken contours giving cause for some uncertainty about the survey data – it is inconceivable that he won't be keeping an eye on the echo sounder. At (D), almost without realising it, he'll get another traditional position check by passing close to the light float.

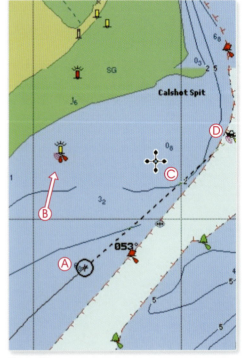

Figure 62

Radar Overlay

One other way of relating the real world to a chart plotter display is to integrate the chart plotter with a radar or vice versa. Some of these combined radar/plotter units are capable of overlaying the radar picture onto the chart (Figure 63).

Figure 63

This makes it relatively easy to pick out which blobs are buoys and which are boats, and which piece of land is which. Almost coincidentally, it's a very good way of checking the GPS and compass, because if either the position or the heading information is wrong, the radar picture won't agree: the radar picture of the coastline will be slightly displaced or rotated compared with the plotter picture that is visible through it.

Summary

- The simplest 'fix' is obtained by passing very close to a fixed and identifiable object.
- Most other fixes involve two or more intersecting position lines:
  - A position line is a line on which you know your position must lie.

GPS

- The Global Positioning System (GPS) provides accurate, worldwide position fixing.
- Most GPS sets can provide other navigation information, including track and velocity, range and bearing to a chosen waypoint and cross-track error.
- GPS positions can easily be plotted on a paper chart using normal plotting instruments, but there are various quick-plotting techniques.

Traditional Position Fixing

- The commonest source of a position line is a visual bearing of a landmark.
  - The bearings of three landmarks, taken in quick succession and plotted on the chart, should intersect to produce a small triangle known as a cocked hat.
  - A good fix is achieved by taking bearings as quickly and accurately as possible using landmarks that can be positively identified and are well-spread around the horizon.
  - Other useful sources of position lines include transits, ranges and contours.

It is almost impossible to spend more than a few hours anywhere on the coast of north-west Europe without becoming aware of the regular rise and fall of sea level, but to boat owners and navigators the tides are especially significant. Fortunately, because tides are an astronomical phenomenon, they are almost as predictable as sunrise and sunset, though their effect can be very different in different parts of the world.

The Half-Daily Pattern – High Waters and Low Waters

Tides are caused primarily by the gravitational pull of the Moon and to a lesser extent by that of the Sun. To understand what's going on it helps to think about them separately, starting with the effect of the Moon.

The common assumption that the Moon orbits the Earth is really something of an oversimplification. In fact, what happens is that the Earth and Moon are held together by each other's gravity, and that this unevenly matched pair spin around their combined centre of mass – a spot called the barycentre, only about 1,000 miles below the surface of the Earth (Figure 64). If you imagine, for a moment, that the Earth is a smooth ball of rock entirely covered by water, then you'll see that the solid Earth is being held in orbit

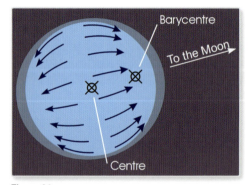

Figure 64

around the barycentre by the gravitational pull of the Moon. The water nearest to the Moon, however, is attracted towards the Moon more strongly than the solid mass of the Earth itself, while the water on the other side is attracted less strongly.

The effect is to form two 'bulges' of water, one on each side of the Earth, rather than the single bulge one might expect.

The Earth, of course, is spinning on its axis every 24 hours, so anyone in a boat anchored at a fixed point on this hypothetical water-covered world would expect to see a 'bulge' roughly once every 12 hours. In practice, however, the interval between High Waters is rather greater than that, because the pattern of bulges and shallows rotates around the Earth in step with the moon, which takes about 27.5 days to complete each orbit. The result is that in every 27.5 days we only get 26.5 days' worth of tides.

That is why High Waters are typically about 12 hours 25 minutes apart, rather than occurring exactly twice a day (Figure 65).

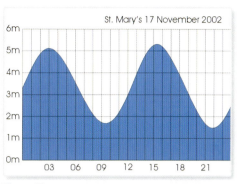

Figure 65

The Half-Monthly Pattern – Springs and Neaps

The Sun also produces tides by exactly the same mechanism. The timing, however, is different. The Sun is also 400 times further away than the Moon, so although it is very much bigger its tide-raising powers are only about 45 per cent of those of the Moon.

The end result is that we don't see the Sun's tides as separate highs and lows. Instead, we see their effect as a distortion of the Moon's tides. Roughly once a fortnight, at about the times of full and new moon, the Sun's tides coincide with those of the Moon to produce spring tides. In between, the Sun and Moon work against each other; the Moon's tides still predominate, but they are reduced to about half the size of a spring tide and are called neap tides. Notice that spring tides have nothing to do with 'spring time'. As the graph in Figure 66 shows, they happen at fortnightly intervals throughout the year – even in November.[10]

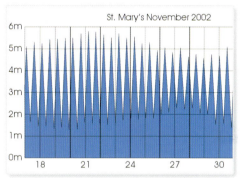

Figure 66

Other Patterns

There are many other, slower rhythms going on in the universe. The distance between the Earth and the Moon changes, as does the distance between the Earth and the Sun, and the angle between the Earth's orbit around the Sun and the Moon's orbit around the Earth. They all have their own distinct cyclical effects on the tides.

One particularly noticeable cycle is that the biggest tides of the year tend to occur around March and September – the so-called Equinoctial Springs – but other patterns take years to repeat themselves.

[10] The tidal graphs in Figures 65, 66, 67 and 68 are based on data supplied by the British Oceanographic Data Centre, part of Proudman Oceanographic Laboratory and funded by DEFRA and the Natural Environment Research Council.

Daily and Half-Daily

Around Europe, we are quite used to the half-daily pattern of tidal highs and lows. In other places this would seem very strange indeed as they have only one tide a day. The reason for this is a combination of two factors.

It is partly caused by the fact that the Moon's orbit around the Earth isn't perpendicular to the spin axis of the Earth. The bulges of water, in other words, don't travel around the Equator. More often, the peak of one bulge

Figure 67

will be anything up to about 25° north of the Equator, while the other is 25° south of it (Figure 67). Someone anchored at a latitude of about 40°N on our hypothetical water-covered world would be quite close to the peak of one bulge (A), but the other bulge (B) would pass nearly 4,000 miles to the south of him, so it would be barely noticeable. In other words, he'd see only one big High Water per day.

So why does the UK see Two Tides per Day?

The reason is that the tides on a water-covered world would be very much smaller than we are used to seeing in real life – less than a metre at their greatest, and probably averaging out to a few centimetres, like those of the Mediterranean. The world's oceans, however, act like great resonators, amplifying the tides in much the same way as the pipes of a church organ amplify the vibrations of the air moving inside them. The Atlantic, being much smaller than the Pacific, resonates to higher frequencies, so (in very general terms) North Atlantic coasts tend to experience the half-daily (semi-diurnal) tidal pattern, while South Pacific coasts experience a more pronounced daily (diurnal) pattern.

Coastal Tides

The resonance of the tides in the oceans has been compared to water sloshing around in a washing-up bowl. Like the sloshing water in a bowl, the level in the middle of a large body of water such as the Atlantic Ocean or the North Sea doesn't actually change very much. Places where this happens are called amphidromic points. There's one in the middle of the North Sea, for instance, about seventy miles east of Lowestoft.

When the tidal 'slosh' gets to the edges, however, the changes of level become very much more noticeable. It behaves, in fact, very much like any other kind of wave reaching a beach: as it runs into shallow water its crest rises, its trough deepens, and its leading edge usually becomes steeper.

Exactly how it changes depends on such a complicated interplay between the tide-raising forces generated by the Sun and Moon and by the shape of the sea bed and coastline that it is almost impossible to predict from theory alone. In some places – of which the Solent (see Figure 68) is just one particularly well-known example – there are so many factors at work that the smooth pattern shown in Figure 65 (St Mary's) is distorted almost beyond recognition. These are sometimes referred to as tidal anomalies, but they aren't really; this apparently anomalous pattern is just an extreme example of the ordinary coastal distortion. That is why, in practice, we use a system of prediction that is based around the idea of standard and secondary ports.

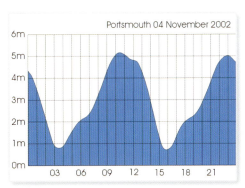

Figure 68

Standard ports are those at which the actual tides have been monitored and recorded carefully over many decades, producing enough data to be 'reverse engineered' to produce mathematical models that can predict future tides. Secondary ports are generally more minor harbours that don't warrant such careful attention; tidal predictions for a secondary port are usually based on less data and on the assumption that the secondary tide is related to the tide at a nearby standard port.

Tide Tables

The world's first computing machines were developed to produce tables showing the predicted rise and fall of the tide. Now, similar calculations can be carried out almost instantaneously by smartphones, yet tide tables are still produced in vast numbers, and are probably the main reason why most yachtsmen buy a new almanac every year.

Standard Ports – High and Low Water

The general layout of a typical set of tide tables for a standard port is shown in Figure 69. This one happens to be Victoria, from the RYA Training Almanac. It shows the time and height of High and Low Water listed every day for a year. From the small extract shown, for instance, we can see that on 2nd August, High Waters occurred at 0353hrs and at 1637hrs, with heights of 4.5 and 4.3 metres above chart datum (see page 40). On the same day, Low Waters were at 1014 and 2247, at 2.0 and 2.3 metres above chart datum.

TIME ZONE **UT**
For Summer Time add ONE hour in **non-shaded areas**

AUGUST

	Time	m		Time	m
1	0259	4.7	**16**	0349	5.0
	0917	1.8		1013	1.5
TH	1533	4.4	F	1630	4.7
	2139	2.1		2240	1.8
2	0353	4.5	**17**	0506	4.7
	1014	2.0		1128	1.8
F	1637	4.3	SA	1750	4.6
	2247	2.3			
3	0501	4.4	**18**	0003	1.8
	1122	2.1		0633	4.6
SA	1753	4.3	SU	1246	1.8
				1907	4.7
4	0002	2.2	**19**	0123	1.7
	0617	4.4		0751	4.7
SU	1232	2.0	M	1354	1.7
	1902	4.5		2012	5.0
5	0111	2.0	**20**	0228	1.5
	0726	4.6		0851	4.9
M	1334	1.8	TU	1449	1.6
	1959	4.7		2102	5.2
6	0209	1.7	**21**	0318	1.3
	0823	4.8		0936	5.0
TU	1427	1.6	W	1532	1.4
	2046	5.0		2143	5.4

Figure 69

A note, in the corner of the page, reminds us that when Summer Time (Daylight Saving Time) is being used we need to add an hour to convert the tabulated times to clock time.

By comparing this tide with the others around it we can see that the afternoon tide is a neap tide, because its range – the difference between High Water and Low Water – is less than that of the tides on 1st August or 3rd August.

This kind of information is certainly useful, up to a point, but it is of limited value if we want to know the depth of water at some other time, or when the tide will reach a specific level.

Standard Ports – Time for a Required Height

To cope with situations like this, a good set of tide tables will include a graph, like that in Figure 71, for each of its standard ports. The right-hand side consists of two graphs, one representing a typical neap tide (the dotted line) and one representing a typical spring tide (the solid line). Every tide is different, but by showing height as a proportion of the total rise or fall of tide (the Factor) these two curves provide sufficient accuracy for most purposes.

The left-hand side of the graph is a ready reckoner, intended to save awkward arithmetic such as 0.53 x 2.3 + 2.0.

Suppose, for instance, that it's 2nd August, and we want to take a RIB *Pirate Sam* to a pontoon in Victoria Harbour, 1.9m above chart datum. *Pirate Sam* needs 0.8m of water to float, so, allowing a safety margin of 0.5m, we reckon we need at least 3.2m of tide. It's often helpful to draw a sketch (like Figure 70) to make sure you're not adding when you should be subtracting, or vice versa.

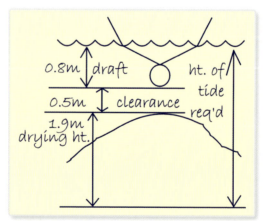

Figure 70

Having worked out the height of tide required, and looked up the details of the day's tide in the tide tables – which in this particular instance shows that Low Water is 2.0m and High Water is 4.3m, at 1014 UT and 1637 UT respectively – the first step in the tidal calculation is to mark the height of Low Water on the Low Water scale, and the height of High Water on the High Water scale, and to join the two with a straight line (steps 1, 2, and 3 in Figure 71).

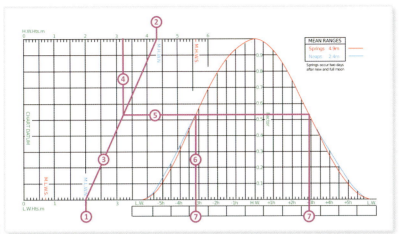

Figure 71

Next, drop a vertical line (4) down from the required height on the High Water scale to meet the diagonal line you've just drawn.

From where they meet draw a horizontal line (5), and from where this horizontal line cuts the graph, draw vertical lines (6) down to the time scale across the bottom (7).

In this case, the answer is that *Pirate Sam* will be able to get to the pontoon any time after 3 hours 10 minutes before High Water until 2 hours 50 after High Water.

Standard Ports – Height at a Specific Time

The ready reckoner really does make the calculation easier, but the mechanics of using it tend to mask what is actually happening. It's rather easier to see what is going on if you work it backwards, to find the height of tide at a specific time.

Suppose, for instance, the question had been "What will be the height of tide in Victoria at 1430 BST on 2nd August?"

High Water is at 1637 UT, or 1737 BST. So 1430 BST is (approximately) 3 hours 10 minutes before HW.

Looking at the graph (Figure 71), and drawing a line upwards from 3h 10m before HW, we can see that it cuts the curve at a point corresponding to a factor of about 0.53 (reading from the Factor scale running vertically up the middle of the graph).

What this means is that the tide has risen 53 per cent of the way from Low Water to High Water. The tide tables tell us that Low Water is 2.0m and High Water is 4.3m, so a factor of 1.00 (100 per cent) would correspond to a rise of 2.3m.

Fifty-three per cent of 2.3m is 1.2. This, however, is the rise above Low Water, so we need to add it to the height of Low Water to get the height of tide above chart datum. The answer, in other words, is 1.2 + 2.0 = 3.2m.

Of course, you don't have to do the calculation like this: the ready reckoner will work just as well backwards as it does forwards.

Tide Reminder

When will the Tide Reach a Particular Height?

1. Mark the height of Low Water on the Low Water scale.
2. Mark the height of High Water on the High Water scale.
3. Join the two marks with a straight line.
4. Find the required height on the High Water scale and draw a vertical line from it.
5. Where line 4 meets line 3, draw a horizontal line.
6. Where line 5 meets the graph, draw a vertical line to the time scale (across the bottom of the graph).

How High will the Tide be at a Particular Time?

Carry out steps 1–3 above.

7. Find the relevant time on the scale across the bottom of the graph, and draw a vertical line up from it.
8. Where line 7 meets the curve, draw a horizontal line.
9. Where line 8 meets line 3, draw a vertical line upwards to the height scale.

Hints

- Draw a diagram to summarise the situation and make sure you are asking yourself the right question.
- Don't forget to correct for local time zones or British Summer Time.
- If it is a spring tide, use the graph drawn in a solid curve.
- If it is a neap tide, use the dotted curve.

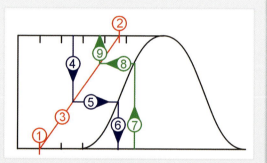

Secondary Ports – High and Low Water

Standard ports are generally important commercial or military harbours. They are not necessarily the kind of places that yachtsmen or motor boaters are most likely to choose to use. The overwhelming majority of harbours and anchorages – particularly the smaller, more attractive ones – don't justify the resources required to produce full tide tables.

Instead, relatively short periods of tidal observation are used to produce tables of differences, which show how the tides at each of these secondary ports differ from those at a nearby standard port.

Figure 72 shows a set of difference tables for Jackson Bay, along with an extract from the tide tables for its standard port of Colville.

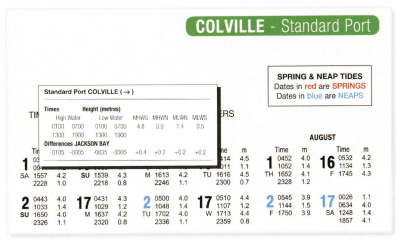

Figure 72

Everyone finds the difference tables confusing at first sight, but it may help to think of them as being divided into two halves:

- The left-hand half deals with times, and is made up of two pairs of columns. One pair is headed High Water; the other pair is headed Low Water. The columns are headed 0100/1300 and 0700/1900 in the High Water side, and 0100/1300 and 0700/1900 in the Low Water side.
- The right-hand half deals with Heights, and it too is divided into two pairs of columns. The High Water columns are labelled MHWS and MHWN, while the Low Water columns are labelled MLWN and MLWS.

The tables in Figure 72, in other words, could equally well be laid out like this:

	Times				Height (metres)			
	High Water		Low Water		High Water		Low Water	
	0100 1300	0700 1900	0100 1300	0700 1900	MHWS 4.8	MHWN 3.9	MLWN 1.4	MLWS 0.5
JACKSON BAY	-0105	-0005	-0035	-0005	+0.4	+0.2	+0.2	+0.2

The revised layout should be clearer, even though it contains exactly the same information. It shows, for instance, that if Low Water Colville is at 0100hrs or 1300hrs, Low Water Jackson Bay is at -0035 – meaning 35 minutes earlier – but if Low Water Colville is at 0700hrs or 1900hrs, Low Water Jackson Bay is at -0005 – meaning 5 minutes earlier.

Similarly, the height columns show that if High Water Colville is 4.8 metres, High Water Jackson Bay is 0.4m higher, but if High Water Colville is 3.9 metres, the difference is reduced to 0.2m.

The first step in using this information must be to find the relevant information for the Standard Port. Suppose, for instance, that we want to find the tidal information for Jackson Bay on 17 August:

The difference tables refer to Colville, whose own tide tables give us:

HW	0634	4.0m
LW	1248	1.4m

The time of HW Colville isn't far off 0700hrs, so it makes sense to use the 0700hrs difference figure for Jackson Bay: -0005.

So High Water Jackson Bay is at 0634 - 0005 = 0629

The height of HW Colville is 4.0m, so it makes sense to use the column headed 3.9m, showing a height difference of +0.2m.

So High Water Jackson Bay is 4.0m + 0.2m = 4.2m above chart datum.

The procedure for Low Water is exactly the same, except that the figures differ:

LW Colville	1248	1.4m
Differences Jackson Bay	- 0035	+0.2m
LW Jackson Bay	1213	1.6m

The differences between a secondary port and its standard port are usually fairly small.

Sometimes, though, the differences are quite marked, and call for some care in the way they are applied.

The first common mistake is to misread the information. At Jackson Bay the Low Water time correction of '0105', for instance, does not mean 105 minutes: it means 1 hour and 5 minutes. It is written that way to conform to the standard navigational practice of writing times as four figures, without the colon between the hours and minutes that appears in bus and train timetables.

The other snag is that big differences are often associated with big differences between the differences. For instance:

If HW Colville is at 1300hrs, HW Jackson Bay is 1h 05m earlier, but if HW Colville is at 1900, HW Jackson Bay is only 05m earlier.

Suppose, however, that on the day we are planning to visit Jackson Bay, HW Colville is 1600.

Neither of the published figures really applies. Common sense, however, suggests that if today's tide is halfway between the tides for which we do have information, then the correction will also be halfway between the published corrections.

This process is called **interpolation**, and many people find they can make perfectly reasonable guesses at the right answer. If you want to be more formal about it, or are striving for great precision or authority, there are three methods in common use:

Interpolation

Arithmetical

We have to assume that the change in the difference is directly proportional to the change in the main value. When the time of High Water Colville changes from 0700hrs to 1300hrs, the difference at Jackson Bay changes from -05 minutes to 1 hour 05 minutes. In other words, the difference has changed by 60 minutes while the time of High Water has changed by 6 hours. So we assume that for every 1 hour change in the time of High Water, the difference changes by 10 minutes.

So if HW Colville is at 1100hrs instead of 1300hrs, it is 2 hours earlier, which means that the difference should have reduced by 20 minutes, from 1 hour 05 minutes to 45 minutes.

Graphical

An alternative method involves drawing a sketch graph, like the one shown in Figure 73, showing how the difference changes. This is particularly useful for time interpolation, which can seem particularly confusing.

Here, for instance, it is easy to see that if HW Colville is at 1100hrs the correction will be about 45 minutes, simply by reading it from the graph.

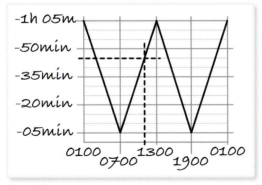

Figure 73

Geometrical

This is quicker and generally as accurate as the graphical method, but it is easy to make significant mistakes – such as getting the change in the differences the wrong way round.

Draw a horizontal line and mark off one set of values – such as time of day or height at standard port – along it (Figure 74). The scale can be anything you like: it could be based on the latitude scale of the chart you happen to be using, or the width of a piece of chewing gum. It doesn't matter what the unit of measurement is, so long as the intervals are regular!

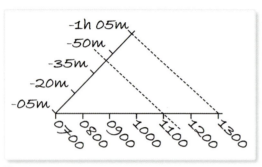

Figure 74

Draw another line at an angle to it and mark that off at regular intervals too, labelling the marks with the thing you are trying to interpolate – in this case, time differences. Make sure that the two marks at the point of the triangle correspond: in this instance that the difference shown of -05min corresponds with the High Water time of 0700hrs.

Finally, use a plotting instrument to draw the third side of the triangle (shown dotted in Figure 74). Draw another line parallel to this one but passing through the time in which you are interested, and the answer will be where that line cuts the sloping scale of differences.

Here, the dotted line that passes through 1100hrs on the time scale cuts the differences scale at -45 minutes.

Secondary Ports – Intermediate Times and Heights

Tide curves are not usually published for secondary ports so unless you are dealing with one of the exceptions (such as Swansea or Dunkirk), the best one can do is to work out the times of High and Low Water and then use the tide curve for the relevant standard port, accepting that the results achieved will be less accurate.

The Rule of Twelfths

The Rule of Twelfths is a simple arithmetical process for estimating the height of tide between High and Low Water. It is less accurate than using the published tide curves but produces reasonable estimates in ports that are reasonably close to open ocean – those whose tidal curves are a smooth, symmetrical bell shape. It should not be used in areas where the tidal curve is distorted by islands or shallow water, such as the Solent and the Dutch and Belgian coasts.

In the 1st hour after High or Low Water, the tide falls or rises one-twelfth of its range.

In the 2nd hour it falls or rises two-twelfths of its range.

In the 3rd hour it falls or rises three-twelfths of its range.

In the 4th hour it falls or rises three-twelfths of its range.

In the 5th hour it falls or rises two-twelfths of its range.

In the 6th hour it falls or rises one-twelfth of its range.

A simpler version of the Rule of Twelfths could be called the Rule of Quarters because it says:

In the first two hours after High or Low Water, the tide falls or rises a quarter of its range.

In the middle two hours it falls or rises half of its range.

In the last two hours it falls or rises a quarter of its range.

Tide Prediction Software

The convoluted arithmetic involved in tidal calculations has been the bane of the lives of thousands of navigation students (and their instructors) for generations. Over recent years, however, the computing power available in PCs, laptops and even mobile phones has increased to such an extent that they can replicate many of the functions carried out by the computers that calculate published tide tables. Several companies produce tidal prediction software at relatively low prices, while others (including the UK Hydrographic Office) offer similar facilities in interactive websites.

These programs are generally easy to use, requiring no more input from the user than the date and port for which you require information, and generally offer a choice of numerical data or graphs, but they seldom produce exactly the same answers as printed tables. Times of High and Low Water in particular seldom agree to the exact minute. Even so, their accuracy is generally quite good enough for everyday purposes, and their reliability is probably better than that of a tired navigator working his or her way through a complicated procedure by numbers.

Meteorological Factors

Whilst the astronomical factors that control the tides are absolutely predictable many years ahead, the weather is not. Unfortunately, meteorological factors can have a distinct effect on the tides. In particular, high barometric pressure can lower the sea level, whilst unusually low pressure can raise it.

The other noticeable factor is that an onshore wind, or one that is being funnelled up an estuary, tends to push the water with it, producing High Waters that are slightly earlier and higher and Low Waters slightly later than might be expected.

The weather doesn't usually cause big variations in sea level. Its effects are in the order of 0.1m for every 10 millibars of barometric pressure change and seldom amount to more than about 0.3m. Occasionally, however, wind, pressure, tide and geography combine to produce surges or storm surges that can raise or lower sea level by a metre or more, and change the times of High and Low Water by an hour or more.

Tidal Streams

It's pretty obvious that raising sea level by several metres across thousands of square miles requires a colossal quantity of water to be brought into the area – and that lowering it again when the tide starts to fall requires an equally large quantity of water to be removed.

Inevitably, then, the vertical movements known as tides involve horizontal movements known as tidal streams. The mere fact that the tide is generally rising at Portsmouth while it falls at Plymouth, however, does not mean that there is a steady east-going current in the English Channel while the tide falls at Plymouth, or a west-going one when the tide rises in Plymouth and falls in Portsmouth.

Such simple 'rectilinear' tidal streams – flowing first one way then the other – do occur in real life, but they are mainly confined to areas such as river estuaries and harbour entrances, where there is a clearly defined channel in which the water can only flow in or out. In most places, though, the tidal streams are classed as rotary, meaning that the direction changes through 360°.

Sources of Information

There are two main sources of tidal stream information:[11] tidal diamonds, printed on charts, and tidal stream atlases, published as separate books and included in miniature form in most yachtsmen's almanacs. Some pilot books also include tidal stream information but it is usually in fairly general terms and intended to warn of areas where the tidal stream poses a particular hazard.

Tidal Diamonds

Tidal diamonds are so called because they refer to diamond-shaped symbols printed on Admiralty charts in magenta ink. Other publishers use other symbols, but the name and the principle are the same.

Each diamond is marked with a letter, which corresponds with a particular part of a data panel printed elsewhere on the chart in which the tidal stream data are presented in numerical form.

Although the relationship between tides and tidal streams is more subtle and complicated than it may appear, it is certainly true that tides and tidal streams are created by the same astronomical forces, so they share a common rhythm. This means that, instead of referring to clock times, the data given in the tidal diamonds can be referred to the time of High Water at a particular port.

Under each diamond heading, the information is divided into three columns and thirteen rows. Each row corresponds to a particular hour before or after High Water. The first column shows the direction towards which the tide is flowing. The second shows its rate (in knots) at a typical spring tide, while the final column shows the rate at that stage in a neap tide.

---

[11] Some navigators refer to the 'set and drift' of a tidal stream. Strictly speaking, set and drift refer to the direction and distance an object would move due to the combined effects of tidal stream, river current and wind-driven surface drift. It would seem an academic distinction, except that drift refers to distance, and rate refers to speed.

In Figure 75, for instance, the section referring to tidal diamond P shows that one hour after HW Victoria, the tidal stream at 45° 47'.6N 5° 54'.3W (the position of the tidal diamond) is flowing in a 302°(T) direction, and that it achieves a rate of 1.5 knots at a typical spring tide, and 0.8 knots at a typical neap tide.

		Tidal Streams referred to HW at VICTORIA														
Hours	Geographical Position	45°56'0N 5 42·2W		45°52'6 N 5 59·4W		45°49'3 N 6 20·4W		45°48'2 N 5 47·2W		45°47·6N 5 54·3W		
Before High Water 6	Directions of streams (degrees)	Rates at spring tides (knots)	Rates at neap tides (knots)	289	2·5 1·3	334	1·2 0·6	355	1·6 0·8	310	4·1 2·0	294	0·9 0·6	00
5				298	1·6 0·9	135	0·9 0·5	357	0·9 0·5	312	3·1 1·6	099	0·8 0·5	01
4				026	0·8 0·5	139	1·4 0·7	172	0·8 0·4	314	2·2 1·2	096	1·4 0·7	02
3				101	1·9 1·0	142	1·3 0·7	175	1·9 1·0	124	2·4 1·3	087	1·2 0·6	18
2				119	2·9 1·5	145	0·9 0·5	179	2·6 1·4	129	4·5 2·3	079	0·9 0·5	17
1				110	3·2 1·7	325	1·0 0·6	182	2·4 1·3	134	5·4 2·7	286	1·1 0·6	17
High Water				109	2·4 1·2	329	1·6 0·8	184	1·8 0·9	126	4·7 2·4	291	1·3 0·7	17
After High Water 1				102	1·6 0·9	329	1·6 0·8	186	1·2 0·7	120	3·7 1·9	302	1·5 0·8	16
2				098	0·9 0·5	332	1·8 0·9	331	0·8 0·4	128	3·4 1·7	308	1·6 0·8	16
3				286	1·1 0·6	334	2·0 1·1	338	1·4 0·7	309	2·6 1·4	307	2·2 1·2	01
4				291	2·0 1·1	333	1·7 0·9	349	1·9 1·0	306	3·8 1·9	303	2·4 1·3	01
5				298	3·3 1·7	331	1·5 0·8	351	2·4 1·3	303	5·2 2·6	298	1·8 0·9	00
6				296	3·2 1·6	332	1·3 0·7	354	2·0 1·1	307	4·8 2·4	296	1·2 0·6	00

Figure 75

Tidal diamonds give the impression of being very precise. Here, for instance, the direction is given as 302°, rather than 'about 300°'. Unfortunately, that impression is somewhat misleading because the tidal stream varies in direction between springs and neaps as well as in its rate. It isn't terribly helpful either, because the information is only valid for a particular moment in each tidal cycle, and for the exact position indicated by the tidal diamond.

Tidal Stream Atlases

Tidal stream atlases provide exactly the same data as tidal diamonds, but in pictorial form, as a sequence of twelve or thirteen small charts, each showing the situation at a particular moment in the tidal cycle. Arrows are used to show the direction of the tidal streams: thick arrows depict strong flows and smaller, thinner arrows depict weaker ones. Greater precision is provided by numbers, such as 08.15 – meaning that the neap rate is 0.8 knots and the spring rate is 1.5 knots, at the position indicated by the dot that separates the two numbers.

These positions usually correspond to the positions of tidal diamonds on the corresponding chart. In Figure 76, the 08.15 north-east of Dawson corresponds exactly with the tidal diamond P in the chart extract in Figure 75.

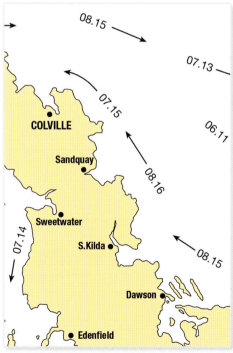

Figure 76

Interpolating between Springs and Neaps

The tide is only a spring or a neap on one day in every seven. For the other six out of seven it will be somewhere in between. In most cases a simple mental approximation is good enough; if you are midway between springs and neaps, take the average of the spring rate and the neap rate. If you are nearer neaps than springs, take a figure rather nearer to the neap rate, and so on.

If higher precision is needed, each Admiralty Tidal Stream Atlas includes an interpolation diagram complete with instructions for its use.

Interpolating for Position

Suppose we are at the position marked with a cross in Figure 77 – exactly midway between the tidal diamonds N and P referred to in the chart extract in Figure 75. The time is 1 hour after HW Victoria.

Which diamond should we use? It could make quite a difference, because at a spring tide the tidal stream at N is 120°, 3.7kn, and at P it is 302°, 1.5kn.

It is tempting to take the average of the data given for the two tidal diamonds:

Figure 77

120° + 302° = 422°
422° ÷ 2 = 211°
and
3.7 + 1.5 = 5.2
5.2 ÷ 2 = 2.6 knots

Think of the situation geographically and visualise a floating object drifting 120° at 3.7 knots for half an hour and north-westwards at 1.5kn for half an hour. After the first half hour, it would have moved about 1.8 miles south-east, but in the second half hour it would drift about 0.7 mile north-westwards.

After an hour it would only have moved about 1.1 mile south-eastwards.

Looking at the shape of the coastline and trying to visualise the way the water would swirl around it suggests that the second answer is probably more realistic, but of course we have no way of saying for sure that it is correct.

The moral is that you need to be very careful when interpolating for positions between two or three tidal diamonds, particularly if there is an obstruction between them or a marked change in direction. It is usually better to make a common-sense estimate based on the Tidal Stream Atlas and to bear in mind that it may not be correct. You will be doing well to estimate within 10 per cent of the rate and 10° of the direction.

Interpolating for Time

Strictly speaking, each slice of data from a tidal diamond, or each picture in a tidal stream atlas, is a snapshot of a precise moment in time and conditions can be expected to change gradually from that moment until the next snapshot an hour later.

In practice, though, we very rarely need to know what the tide is doing at a particular moment; we are usually much more interested in what its effect will be over a period of time.

The conventional approach – and one that works well for almost all purposes – is to assume that each snapshot is valid for a period extending from half an hour before its time to half an hour after.

In other words, if High Water Victoria is at 1713 UT, the Tidal Stream Atlas page labelled "One hour after HW Victoria" is really valid only at 1813hrs, but we treat it as valid from 1743hrs to 1843hrs.

If you are likely to be using tidal stream data a lot, such as if you are navigating by EP (see page 110), it may be worth adjusting the timing of your navigational routine so that you plot positions etc. at times that fit in neatly with the tidal cycle.

If, however, you really need to know what the tide is doing from 1800hrs to 1900hrs, the textbook solution is to take 43 minutes' worth of the data relating to 1813hrs, (because it is accepted as valid from 1743hrs to 1843hrs, so we are going to use it for the period from 1800hrs to 1843hrs) and 17 minutes' worth of the data relating to 1913hrs (because it is accepted as valid from 1843hrs to 1943hrs, of which we are only interested in the period from 1843hrs to 1900hrs).

It cannot be stressed too often, though, that this is all based on assumptions and estimates, which are themselves based on predictions which may not be 100 per cent accurate. Don't let the apparent precision of the arithmetic lead you into the trap of believing that the answers are necessarily right!

Summary

- Tides are the predictable rise and fall of the sea caused primarily by the forces of gravity between the Earth, Moon and Sun. They are distorted by local geography.
  - Tides with a larger than average range are called springs.
  - Tides with a smaller than average range are called neap tides, and occur at fortnightly intervals a few days after each quarter moon.

Tide Tables
- Tide tables are available for many 'standard ports' around the world.
  - Good-quality tide tables also include a graph showing how the height of tide changes between high and low water.
  - Difference tables can be used to estimate the tidal information for smaller 'secondary ports' near a standard port.

Tidal Streams
- Raising and lowering sea levels create tidal streams.
- Tidal stream information is available on charts or in tidal stream atlases.
  - On charts, tidal stream data is given by tidal diamonds.
  - In tidal stream atlases, tidal stream data is presented graphically.
    - It is possible to interpolate between the information given to find the tidal stream at tides between springs and neaps, and at intermediate positions and times.

At the end of Chapter 4, the crew of *Proud Maiden* found themselves about a mile from where they expected to be, after only half an hour under way. There are several possible reasons for this, but in tidal waters the tidal stream is a strong probability.

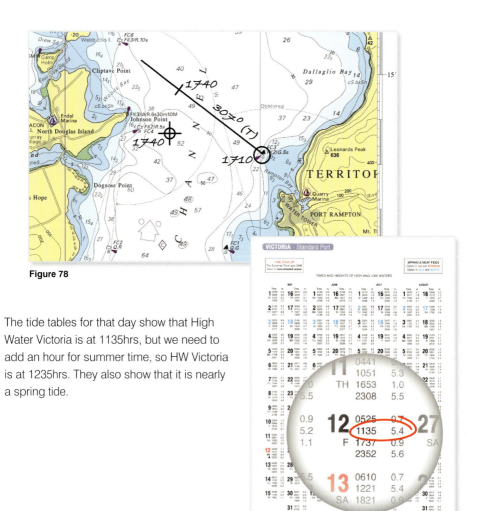

Figure 78

The tide tables for that day show that High Water Victoria is at 1135hrs, but we need to add an hour for summer time, so HW Victoria is at 1235hrs. They also show that it is nearly a spring tide.

The tidal stream data on the chart (Figure 79) shows that at tidal diamond C, there was a fairly strong tidal stream flowing southwards:

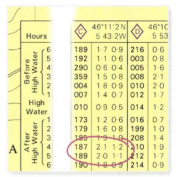

187° 2.1 knots at 1635hrs and

189° 2.0 knots at 1735hrs.

So while *Proud Maiden* has been moving north-westwards through the water, the water itself has been moving south, at about two knots, taking the boat with it.

Figure 79

In half an hour – the time since *Proud Maiden* fixed her position at the buoy in Rampton Bay – the water has covered a mile, so it is hardly surprising that the 1740hrs fix puts her a mile south of her 1740hrs DR position.

The follow-up to this is that her navigator could have counteracted the effect of the tidal stream by initially aiming for a point somewhere up-tide of his intended destination. The question, of course, is how far up-tide should he have aimed?

Using the Track, CoG, or CMG Display

One very simple and direct method of counteracting the effect of tidal streams is provided by most GPS displays. These can show the direction in which you are actually moving – usually called your Track, Course Made Good, or Course over Ground (TRK, CMG, or CoG) – as well as the Bearing to Waypoint (BTW), which represents the direction you want to travel.

In the case of *Proud Maiden's* passage to Douglas Island, for instance, the Bearing to Waypoint would initially have been 307°(T), but her Track, from the fix at 1710hrs to the one at 1740hrs, would have been about 280°(T).

By altering course about 30° to starboard, her navigator could have made the Track and Bearing to Waypoint match. In other words, the boat would have been moving straight along the line marked 307° (T), even though her compass – showing the heading, or the direction in which she is pointing – would have indicated something quite different.

Using the Cross-Track Error Display

An alternative is to monitor the cross-track error display (see pages 72–73). By definition, the cross-track error shows how far you have strayed from the straight-line path from one waypoint to the next, so if you keep it to zero you must be on track. This is the principle behind most autopilots' 'steer to waypoint' function.

Most human helmsmen, though, are inclined to overcorrect for small changes, so it is better not to aim to keep the cross-track error to zero, but to keep it to within a short distance each side. On a short, 5-mile passage, a reasonable target might be a cross-track error of 0.1 mile. On a 50-mile trip, a mile or so would be more realistic.

Finding Course to Steer by Chartwork

A more traditional approach is to calculate the course to steer by geometry, using the chart itself as a worksheet.

Course to Steer for One Hour or Less

The first step is to draw in the intended track as a straight line from your starting point to the intended destination and beyond.

The next is to draw another line, from the same starting point, to represent the tidal stream, pointing in the direction the stream is flowing and with its length proportional to the speed of flow. Figure 80 shows the most traditional approach, in which one minute of latitude represents one knot of tidal stream.

Mathematically, it doesn't matter what scale you use: a knot could be represented by a centimetre, or by an inch, or even by some completely arbitrary unit.

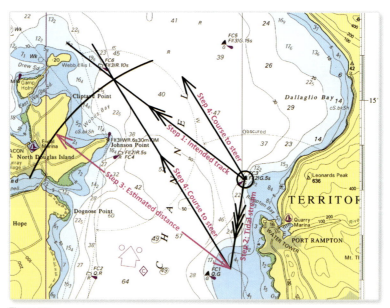

Figure 80

The third step is to open a pair of drawing compasses or dividers to a distance equivalent to the boat speed, using the same scale as the tide speed. Put one point of the dividers or compasses at the end of the tide vector, and use the other to strike an arc across the line that represents the intended track.

Finally, draw a straight line to the point where the arc intersects the intended track. The direction of this line represents the course to steer. It does not matter that it seems to be starting from the wrong place because we are only interested in its direction: the boat won't actually be sailing along the line. Nor does it matter if any of the other lines drawn to calculate the course to steer pass over shallow patches, or hazards, or even cross the coastline: they are only a mathematical construction. The only one that has any direct relationship to the movement of the boat across the surface of the real world is the one representing the intended track.

Course to Steer for Several Hours

All three of the methods described so far are perfectly adequate for relatively short periods of time – up to about an hour, say – in which the tidal stream probably won't change very much. They become progressively less useful over longer periods. The two GPS methods, in particular, cannot possibly take account of future tidal streams.

The principle of the traditional method – of plotting the effect of the tidal stream from the starting point and then drawing an arc centred on the end of the tidal vector – can, however, easily be adapted.

The first stage of the process is exactly the same: it involves drawing the intended track onto the chart as a straight line from the point of departure to the intended destination and beyond (Figure 81).

- The intended track must be a straight line. This method does not allow for hazards.
- The intended track must lie across open water, with a substantial safety margin on each side; despite its name, it does not represent the boat's actual movement over the ground.

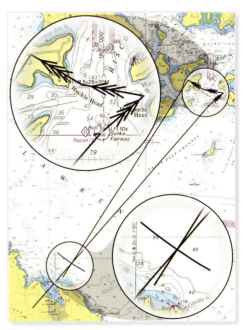

The next stage is to assess the tidal stream that the boat will experience at each hour of the intended passage. Suppose, for instance, that *Fleta* is about to leave Douglas Island, aiming for Colville. Her skipper expects the 16-mile passage from Synka Fairway buoy to take about three hours, so he looks up the tidal streams for the three hours in question – bearing in mind that he expects to be making progress across the channel the whole time. In other words, he looks at the tidal stream arrows just off the island for the first hour, at the arrows halfway across for the second hour and at the arrows just off Colville for the final hour.

Figure 81

It is useful to draw up a simple table, like this:

12:46–13:46	050°	1.2kt
13:46–14:46	280°	1.4kt
14:46–15:46	300°	1.3kt

The tidal stream vectors can then be drawn onto the chart, starting from the intended starting point, but joining onto each other nose to tail as shown in the diagram (Figure 81). As in the simple 1-hour calculation, it does not matter what scale you use: most navigators prefer to stick to the scale of the chart, so a 1.3 knot tidal stream is represented by an arrow 1.3 miles long. There is no reason, however, why you shouldn't use centimetres, quarter-inches, or any other unit you like, so long as you are absolutely consistent throughout the calculation.

The One in Sixty Rule

It's a slightly obscure but very convenient trigonometric fact that the sine of 1° is about 1/60, and that for angles up to about 45°, dividing any angle by sixty gives a reasonable approximation of its sine.

Navigators take advantage of this in all sorts of ways, including working out a course to steer:

$$\frac{\text{Tide speed x 60}}{\text{Boat speed}} = \text{course correction}$$

The course correction is always uptide.

In the example on page 102, *Proud Maiden* experienced a tidal stream of 2 knots, and had a boat speed of 5 knots.

$$\frac{2 \times 60}{5} = \frac{120}{5} = 24°$$

This is true if the tidal stream is roughly at right angles to the intended track. If it is ahead or astern, no offset is required. If it is at about 45° to the intended track, use two-thirds of its rate in the formula instead of its full rate.

In the example on this page, *Fleta* was expecting to be pushed 1.2 miles north-east and 2.7 miles west, in 3 hours.

The 1.2 miles north-east is directly ahead of her. It slows her down but does not push her sideways, so it counts as zero. The 2.7 miles west is at about 45° to the intended track, so it creates 1.8 'miles' worth' of offset.

Overall, the tide pushes her 1.8 miles sideways in 3 hours, equivalent to an average of 0.6 knots.

$$\frac{0.6 \times 60}{5} = \frac{36}{5} = 7° \text{ (approx.)}$$

The third stage is again just a scaled-up version of the 1-hour version: it involves drawing an arc with a radius equivalent to the distance the boat is expected to travel in the time and its centre on the end of the tidal vectors. This is why it may be useful to use something other than the chart scale for the tidal vectors: it may be easy to draw a tidal vector a mile or two long, but it can be difficult to draw the arc of a circle with a radius of perhaps 100 miles or more. It is not unusual to have to improvise, using pieces of string or the edges of other charts instead of compasses.

Finally, join the end of the tidal vector to the point at which the arc cuts the intended track. The direction of this line represents the course to steer.

In this particular example, you can see that the tide changes direction through more than 180° during the course of the passage, pushing *Fleta* north-eastwards during the first hours, but then even more strongly westwards.

Had *Fleta's* navigator relied on the GPS, he would have started his passage steering slightly to starboard (right) of his intended track in order to offset the first hour's tide. In the second half of the passage, by contrast, he would have been steering well off to port (left) to offset the west-going tide. It would have kept him on track but would have taken longer and involved sailing further.

Leeway

Even in still, tideless waters a boat seldom moves in the direction it is pointing. More often it will slide sideways under the influence of the wind, carving out a water track or wake course that may be several degrees downwind of the course indicated by the compass (Figure 82).

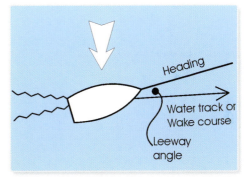

Figure 82

This sideways movement is called leeway.

It's a complex phenomenon, depending on all sorts of variables including the shape of the underwater parts of the hull, the shape of its topsides and superstructure, the strength and direction of the wind and the speed at which the boat is moving. In the case of sailing boats, the sails and rig play an important part, as do any canopies or covers on a motor boat. Less-obvious factors include things such as the depth of water and the sea state.

Leeway can be allowed for in two ways:

- In the Royal Navy, it is usually measured in knots and treated as though it were a tidal stream at right angles to the ship's course.
- Most small-craft navigators express leeway as an angle, and treat it as a correction to the boat's course.

Measuring Leeway

Before you can allow for leeway, however, it must first be either measured or estimated.

It is difficult to do this with any accuracy, particularly in the rough conditions in which it is likely to be greatest. When there is no tidal stream the leeway angle can be measured directly by passing very close to a fixed mark such as a buoy and then, after several minutes, taking a bearing of the buoy. In theory, if you add or subtract 180° from the bearing of the buoy (to get the reciprocal) and then compare the answer with the course steered, the discrepancy is the amount of leeway. Fortunately, perhaps, leeway is usually in the order of only a few degrees – sometimes as much as 20 degrees. Unfortunately, the fact that it is generally small means that a few degrees of helmsman error, a degree or so of deviation on the steering compass and another degree or so on the hand-bearing compass can add up to a significant error in the measurement of leeway by this method.

A better option is to take careful note of the Track/CoG/CMG shown by the GPS, and compare it with the course being steered.

Best of all, though, is to note the boat's position, steer a steady course for an hour or two and note the position again. Then estimate her position using the techniques described on page 110 but assuming no leeway and compare the estimated position with the actual position. Whilst there may be other factors involved, the main element in any discrepancy is likely to be leeway.

The Leeway Formula

Some of the most sophisticated instrument systems appear to measure leeway. What they are actually doing, though, is collecting information from other sensors – particularly the log and inclinometer (measuring how far the boat is heeling over) – and applying the formula:

$$\frac{\text{Heel}}{\text{Speed}^2} \times K = \text{Leeway}$$

K is a constant primarily related to the boat's design that can be found by measuring the leeway in one set of conditions and then put into the formula to calculate leeway in other circumstances. This is not, however, applicable to motor boats.

Leeway in Sailing Boats

Leeway in sailing boats is generally greatest when sailing close-hauled, and reduces to nothing on a dead run. It increases when the boat is reefed, but increases even more if she is allowed to heel excessively. The most extreme leeway occurs when the boat is moving slowly, such as when an inexperienced helmsman 'pinches' (sails too close to the wind) or when the boat is hove-to.

By contrast, many helmsmen – particularly those with experience of racing dinghies – tend to luff up in gusts and bear away in lulls. This is a particularly efficient way of sailing because it helps keep the boat sailing flat and keeps the boat speed up, whilst actually achieving an average course that is slightly closer to the wind than looking at the compass alone suggests. The result is that the leeway angle may appear to be negative. This may be a source of pride for the helmsman, but it doesn't make the navigator's job any easier!

Leeway in Motor Boats

Leeway is caused by the wind, but it is not confined to sailing boats. Many motor boats, in fact, make more leeway than sailing boats because they often have high topsides and superstructures, often with canopies or covers to increase their windage, without the benefit of a keel to help them resist being pushed sideways.

In light and moderate conditions, leeway for a motor boat is greatest when the wind is blowing straight across her course and least when it is dead ahead or directly astern.

That generalisation, however, becomes distorted in fresher conditions, when the helmsman's reactions become more significant. When going downwind, with waves lifting the stern of the boat and then rolling her sideways, a typical slow or medium-speed motor boat has a natural tendency to turn to windward as the stern lifts. At the same time, her speed increases because she is going downhill. As the wave passes underneath the helmsman's corrective action takes effect, so she turns downwind again – but is now moving relatively slowly, on the 'uphill' slope of the wave. The end result is that the average course steered may well be several degrees upwind of the course the helmsman thinks he is steering.

When travelling fast enough to overtake the waves this is much less of a problem. Even novice helmsmen quickly find that this can be reduced by turning away from the wind – apparently increasing the leeway.

Allowing for Leeway

If you know how much leeway your boat is likely to make under any particular set of conditions it can be allowed for simply by adding or subtracting the leeway angle from the course steered (Figure 83).

The easiest way to decide whether leeway should be added or subtracted is to draw a big arrow on the chart, pointing downwind. True leeway always pushes the

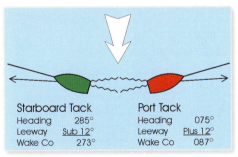

Starboard Tack		Port Tack	
Heading	285°	Heading	075°
Leeway	Sub 12°	Leeway	Plus 12°
Wake Co	273°	Wake Co	087°

Figure 83

boat downwind of her course. Negative leeway, caused by the helmsman steering a different course, is a different matter.

The alternative is to remember that if the wind is from the **starboard** side, leeway needs to be **subtracted** from the course to find the direction the boat is actually moving through the water. If the wind is from the **port** side it has to be **plussed** (added).

Estimating Position

Before electronic position fixing systems such as GPS made it possible to get accurate position information, the estimated position or EP was the cornerstone of navigation when out of sight of land. Its importance has faded, but it is still a valuable technique.

Strictly speaking, an estimated position is based on a DR (Dead Reckoning position: see page 45) adjusted for the estimated effects of leeway, tidal stream, current and surface drift. In practice, in tidal waters, current is included in the tidal stream data, so it requires no special treatment, and surface drift (caused by wind blowing across open water) is generally slight and impossible to estimate with any accuracy.

An everyday EP, in other words, consists of a DR position, corrected for the effects of wind and tide.

A DR position is based solely on the course steered and the distance travelled through the water. It is derived by drawing a straight line from the previous position in the direction of the boat's course and marking off the distance she has travelled (Figure 84).

Figure 84

To correct for the effects of leeway a new line is drawn, representing the wake course or water track. In formal chart-work it is distinguished from the course by the addition of a single arrowhead (Figure 85).

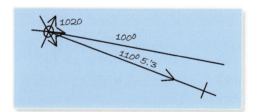

Figure 85

The position obtained by marking the distance travelled along the water track is seldom identified as anything in particular because for most purposes it is just an intermediate step towards an EP. Occasionally, however, it is referred to as the Sea Position.

The Estimated Position is derived from the Sea Position by allowing for the movement of the sea itself, drawing a line from the Sea Position in the direction of the tidal stream and marking off the distance a drifting object would have travelled under the influence of the tidal stream alone (Figure 86).

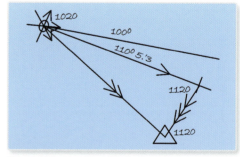

Figure 86

By convention, the tidal stream is represented by three arrowheads and the Estimated Position by a triangle.

Over relatively short periods of time, and so long as the boat has not altered course, the line from her starting position to the EP should correspond quite closely to the direction the boat has moved relative to the sea bed, so it is called her ground track (or just track). In formal chartwork it is identified by two arrows.

In practice, however, most of the lines involved in constructing the EP may be omitted or rubbed out for the sake of clarity; the most important convention is that an EP is marked by a triangle and – like any position – labelled with the time.

Estimating Position – Less than or More than an Hour

The simple example above of working out an Estimated Position involved a time interval of exactly 1 hour between the fix and the subsequent EP. On a long passage it may well be convenient to work up EPs at hourly intervals, because it is a convenient interval that is easily remembered and fits in well with the way tidal stream data is presented (Figure 86).

There is nothing particularly magical about an hour: the principle of an EP is valid whether the time interval is a few minutes or several hours. The key feature is that the tidal stream vectors must relate to the same time interval as the course and speed vectors.

In other words, if you take half an hour's worth of boat movement, you must allow half an hour's worth of tide (Figure 87). If you use 4 hours of boat movement, you must use the same 4 hours' worth of tide – bearing in mind that the tidal stream varies from place to place as well as from time to time.

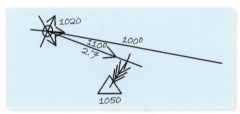

Figure 87

What may seem more surprising is that you do not have to maintain a constant course or speed throughout the time interval in question, so long as your alterations of course and speed are monitored and reflected in the plotting that goes into producing the sea position.

> The convention for labelling the water track, tidal stream and ground track has no relation to the mathematical convention for labelling vectors and their resultants, even though the principle is identical. Some people find it helps to think of dipping A FOOT in the water but standing with BOTH FEET on the ground: one arrow for the water track and two arrows for the ground track.

The technique has some similarity to the processes involved in working out a course to steer over several hours, in that the tidal vectors for each hour are added by being joined together, nose to tail. In other respects, though, it's just a scaled-up version of the 1-hour EP, in that the first stage involves working-up courses and distances to produce the DR (or the Sea Position). Then the tide vectors are added, nose to tail, starting from the DR, and again checking that the

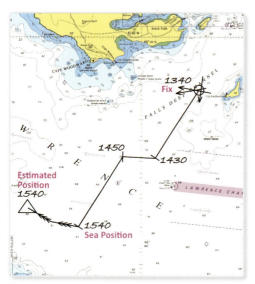

Figure 88

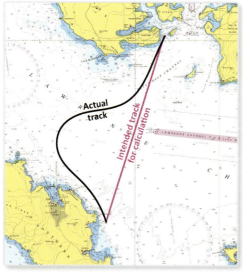

Figure 89

time frames are the same. In the example in Figure 88, for instance, the DR covers the two-hour period from 1340hrs to 1540hrs (including a 20-minute alteration of course between 1430hrs and 1450hrs), so the tidal vectors must apply to the same two hours.

EPs and Cross-Track Error

GPS is very good at telling you where you are. It is not at all good at telling you whether that is where you ought to be, particularly if you have worked out a course to steer to counteract the effect of several hours' worth of constantly changing cross-tide.

In Figure 89, for instance, the workboat *Mabel Stanley* has set off from Sandquay to tow a dismasted keelboat to Dunbarton. The tow limits her speed to about two knots, so her skipper expects the 18-mile trip to take about eight or nine hours. With tidal streams that sometimes flow faster than his boat speed, he has carefully calculated his course to steer: it's almost ten degrees to port of the straight-line route because the eastgoing tidal stream in the second half of the passage will be stronger than the westgoing stream in the first half.

This, however, means that for the first half of the passage his course and the tidal stream are working together to push *Mabel Stanley* further and further west of the rhumb line.

Looking at Figure 90 (on page 113), we can see that this is only to be expected – but for the skipper, steering 010° while the GPS tells him that the Bearing to Waypoint is 045° and the cross-track error is 5 miles and increasing, it may not be so obvious.

In this sort of situation, plotting an Estimated Position provides valuable reassurance.

So long as you have confidence in your ability to predict your boat speed reasonably accurately it can even be done in advance, to show what the cross-track error should be at each stage of the passage.

Pools of Errors

Even the most carefully calculated EP is exactly what its name suggests – an estimate.

All sorts of things conspire to make it wrong:

- Errors in the initial fix.
- Compass and steering errors.
- Too much (or too little) allowance for leeway.
- Log error.
- Errors in the tidal stream data.
- Factors ignored or unaccounted for (such as surface drift).
- Plotting errors.

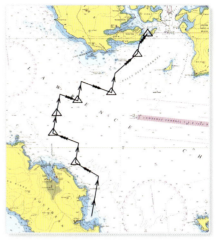

Figure 90

Most of these errors are always present to some extent, but their effect changes from time to time. Suppose, for instance, that the boat's log under-reads by 10 per cent. At the moment you take a fix this doesn't matter. If you were to plot an EP after you had travelled 3 miles, the fact that the log showed you had only travelled 2.7 miles would produce an error of 0.3 miles. Ten miles from the fix, the error has grown to 1 mile... and so on.

Figure 91 is a redrawn, and rather more accurate, version of Figure 86, in which the magenta spot around the fix represents the area of uncertainty.

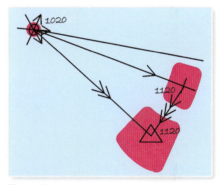

Figure 91

If there were no log or compass errors, no leeway and no helmsman's errors, the Sea Position, an hour later, would be a spot the same size. In reality, though, it has grown, getting wider because of possible directional errors and longer because of possible distance errors.

In plotting the tidal stream, too, there are likely to be errors in both its direction and rate, so the area of uncertainty expands still more.

Like a puddle of water that gets bigger as water flows into it, this pool of errors expands as the errors themselves develop.

Every so often, though, the pool shrinks. A GPS fix, for instance, immediately reduces it to a circle a few metres in diameter. Crossing a contour reduces it to a narrow ribbon, along the contour, while a transit reduces it to a short straight line.

Very few navigators, in everyday life, even attempt to quantify the errors or to plot the limits of the pool of errors. It is worth keeping the idea of the pool of errors at the back of your mind, however, and being constantly aware that you are almost certainly not at the pinpoint position you have just marked on the chart, but are really somewhere inside an ever-expanding pool – usually portrayed as circular or oval in shape, but really more of an ill-defined blob.

Errors

The size of any error is likely to depend on the boat, the conditions, the equipment and the skill of the individual navigator.

The following table is a rough guide to the sort of accuracies that can be achieved on board a typical yacht.

Sea state	Smooth	Moderate	Rough
GPS fix	15m	15m	15m
Visual bearing	±2°	±5°	±10°
Transit	±0.2°	±0.2°	±0.5°
Echo sounder	±5 per cent	±5 per cent	±5 per cent
Steering	±2°	±5°	±10°
Log (sail)	±2 per cent	±5 per cent	±10 per cent
Log (power)	±5 per cent	±5 per cent	±10 per cent
Tidal stream (set)	±10°	±10°	±10°
Tidal stream (rate)	±20 per cent	±20 per cent	±20 per cent
Radar range	±2°	±2°	±2°

Summary

- Over short distances, the effect of a tidal stream pushing the boat sideways can be offset by using GPS:
- Either steer so that the track matches the bearing to waypoint
  or
- steer to keep the cross-track error small.

Course to Steer
- Over longer distances, it is better to calculate the course to steer based on the predicted tidal streams and estimated boat speed.
- Leeway is the extent to which a boat is pushed sideways by the action of the wind.
  - If you have a reasonable idea of how much leeway your boat makes, you can allow for it by arithmetic:
    - On starboard tack, subtract the leeway to find the 'wake course'.
    - On port tack, add the leeway to find the 'wake course'.

Estimated Position
- An Estimated Position (EP) is based on a dead reckoning, corrected for leeway and tidal streams or currents.

9 | LIGHTS, BUOYS & BEACONS

The Pharos of Alexandria was one of the seven wonders of the ancient world and remained so for over 1,500 years. It was probably the first proper lighthouse, consisting of a tower 117 metres high with a mirror at the top to focus the light from a wood-burning fire, to make it visible from up to 35 miles away.

By comparison, Créac'h lighthouse, just off the north-western tip of France, is the brightest lighthouse of the modern world: it is 70m high, and has a nominal range of 33 miles.

But although lighthouses haven't got bigger or brighter over the past couple of millennia they have certainly multiplied in numbers and have become very much more sophisticated. There are also countless smaller navigation marks, including smaller lighthouses and beacon towers, solar-powered buoys and beacons, and unlit buoys, right down to withies – little more than crudely trimmed tree branches stuck in the mud – which are still used to mark some minor channels.

Lighthouses

The whole purpose of a lighthouse is to be seen, so its luminous range or visible range – the distance at which it can be seen – is a pretty key feature. Unfortunately, the visible range is not something which can really be printed on charts or included in reference books, because it depends on three completely unrelated factors:

- The brightness of the light.
- Its height and the observer's height of eye.
- The weather conditions at the time.

The upshot of this is that the distance at which you can expect to see a light will be whichever is least of its geographical range and its nominal range, both adjusted for weather conditions if necessary.

Nominal Range

Lighthouse engineers specify the power of a lighthouse in candelas (or candlepower). This is a much better unit to use for the job than the watts or kilowatts that one might expect because it is a direct measure of the intensity of the light rather than of the energy expended in producing it. Unfortunately, the definition of a candela is meaningless to most of us, and the idea of a light 'equivalent to 500,000 candles' is hardly any better.

Nor is the intensity of a light directly related to its range. A 10m yacht, for instance, can meet the requirement to carry a masthead light that is visible for 2 miles with just 4.3 candela. The corresponding light on a large ship has to be at least 94 candelas to meet its legal minimum of 6 miles, whilst the half-million candelas of a fairly typical major lighthouse is good for a nominal range of only 24 miles.

To overcome these problems, navigators – and the books and charts on which we rely – are more likely to refer to brightness in terms of a light's nominal range (Figure 92). This is defined as the luminous (visible) range of the light in meteorological visibility of 10 miles, assuming the observer's height of eye is sufficient for the light to be above his horizon.[12]

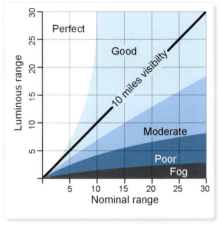

The practical effect of this is that a yacht navigator, with a relatively low vantage point, may not actually see a lighthouse at anything like its nominal range, because at that distance it may well be below his horizon. Nor will it achieve its nominal range if the visibility is poor.

On the other hand, even a low and dim light may sometimes be visible considerably further than its nominal range suggests.

Figure 92

Geographical Range

The geographical range of a light is the greatest distance at which it would be visible above an observer's horizon, assuming that it is bright enough and weather conditions permit. In other words, it is exactly the same as the dipping distance referred to in Chapter 6 (see page 82).

Meteorological Factors

Strictly speaking, both nominal and geographical ranges need to be adjusted to account for weather conditions.

The most obvious of these is the visibility, whose effect is shown in the chart above (Figure 92), but it is worth bearing in mind that weather conditions can also affect the way in which light rays travel through the atmosphere.

Even under so-called 'normal' conditions, the assumption that light travels in straight lines is misleading: it bends very slightly to follow the curvature of the Earth's surface. This effect – known as refraction – usually increases the geographical range by between 5 per cent and 10 per cent of its theoretical value.

Occasionally, however, particularly in areas of high atmospheric pressure or when the air temperature is much higher than the temperature of the water surface, refraction increases,

[12] The meteorological conditions used for calculating the intensity of lights shown by vessels under the collision regulations are slightly different (equivalent to a visibility of 13 miles).

increasing the range at which lights become visible. When the air temperature is much lower than the sea temperature the opposite happens and the rays of light may even bend away from the surface, reducing the geographical range to its theoretical value or even less.

Light Characteristics

The light of the Pharos of Alexandria probably varied considerably in both intensity and colour, but perhaps the most significant difference between modern lighthouses and their ancient ancestor is that these two features can now be varied deliberately to give each lighthouse its own distinctive characteristics. In particular, the light can be flashed or obscured to produce a distinctive rhythm, the time taken to complete each sequence of flashes can be varied to give a distinctive period, and the colour can be chosen or altered.

Rhythm

The simplest possible rhythm is no rhythm at all – the light is displayed continuously and unvaryingly, so it is classified as fixed (F on charts). Unfortunately, most of the other artificial lights around us are also fixed, so it would be difficult to pick out a navigation mark showing a fixed light against a background of street lights, house lights, advertising signs and even low stars. For this reason, where fixed lights are used for navigation marks they are generally confined to relatively minor roles, such as marking the ends of jetties and pontoons – and even then they are generally given a distinctive colour such as red or green, and are often mounted in pairs, one above the other. On large-scale harbour plans, for instance, it is quite common to see jetty heads marked with the abbreviation 2FR(vert), meaning 'two fixed red lights, vertically disposed'.

More important lights usually have more sophisticated rhythms, mostly falling into one of two main groups:

- Flashing.   • Occulting.

Flashing

A flashing light, in everyday language, means simply going on and off, but in navigational terminology the definition is rather more precise. It means that the intervals of darkness are longer than the duration of the flashes.[13] On charts, flashing lights can be recognised by the abbreviation Fl.

The flashes may be regularly spaced, in which case the light is described simply as flashing, or they may be split up into groups, with two or more flashes in quick succession, separated by a longer interval of darkness. These group flashing lights are commonly used for major lighthouses and can be recognised on charts by a number in brackets indicating the number of flashes in each group – such as Fl(5) for the Casquets lighthouse (just west of Alderney) and Fl(3) for Start Point lighthouse (between Salcombe and Dartmouth).

---

[13] In reality, flashing lights do not always go on and off. In big lighthouses in particular the appearance of flashing is produced by using mirrors or lenses to focus the light into one or more beams that sweep around the horizon.

Fixed	F	Unchanging	
Flashing	Fl	Less light than dark	
Group flashing	Fl (2)	(for example)	
Composite group flashing	Fl (2+1)	(for example)	
Long flashing	LFl	Flash lasting more than 2 seconds	
Quick	Q	50–79 flashes per min	
Group quick	Q (9)	(for example)	
Very quick	VQ	80–159 flashes per min	
Interrupted very quick	IVQ	IVQ	

━━━ = ONE SEQUENCE

Less often, the flashes may be divided into several distinct groups, in which case the rhythm is described as composite group flashing. A light showing a pair of flashes, followed by a longer interval of darkness before a group of three flashes, for instance, would be described as composite group flashing 2+3 – abbreviated on a chart to Fl(2+3).

If a flash lasts longer than 2 seconds it is known, logically enough, as a long flash, and is abbreviated to L Fl.

Other variations on this theme can be achieved by varying the rate at which the flashes appear. Between 50 and 79 flashes per minute – about the same as a car's indicator lights – is known as quick flashing or just quick, while 80 to 159 flashes per minute is known as very quick. Their abbreviations are Q and VQ respectively. Lights flashing faster than this are relatively rare, but they are used occasionally, in which case they are known as ultra-quick, abbreviated to UQ.

Quick and very quick lights can show distinct groups of flashes, just like flashing lights. They are often used for cardinal buoys but you will sometimes come across something that looks like a group quick or group very quick, but for which the number of flashes in each group is not specified. It is described instead as an interrupted quick (IQ) or interrupted very quick (IVQ). In the case of ultra-quick lights, where the flashes follow each other too quickly to count, this interrupted ultra-quick (IUQ) is really the only practical variation.

Occulting

An occulting light also goes on and off,[14] but in this case the periods of light are longer than the intervening occultations (or occlusions).

Like flashes, occlusions can be arranged to happen at regular intervals, or in groups, or in composite groups, abbreviated to Oc, or (for instance) Oc(3) or Oc(2+1). The rate at which the occlusions occur can also be varied, but the terms quick, very quick and ultra-quick are not applied.

---

[14] As with flashing lights, the lamp of an occulting light is often permanently lit. Its characteristic rhythm is produced by moving screens or shutters.

Other Rhythms

There are yet more variations that can be applied to the rhythms of lights, apparently limited only by the ingenuity of the people who design them and the complexity of the waters they are required to mark.

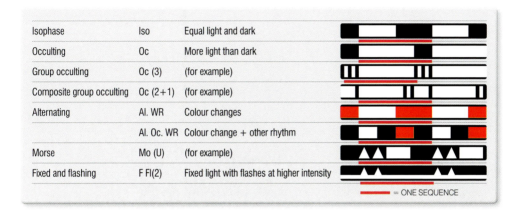

Isophase	Iso	Equal light and dark	
Occulting	Oc	More light than dark	
Group occulting	Oc (3)	(for example)	
Composite group occulting	Oc (2+1)	(for example)	
Alternating	Al. WR	Colour changes	
	Al. Oc. WR	Colour change + other rhythm	
Morse	Mo (U)	(for example)	
Fixed and flashing	F Fl(2)	Fixed light with flashes at higher intensity	

 = ONE SEQUENCE

One of these cannot really be described as either flashing or occulting because it consists of equal intervals of light and dark. These isophase lights are somewhat unusual – their most common application is on 'safe water marks' such as the buoys that are sometimes used to mark the beginning of a buoyed channel.

Alternating lights (Al) are another special case, in which any of the basic rhythms can be varied by changing the colour of the light.

In its simplest form – analogous to a fixed light – an alternating light simply changes colour, flicking between white and red for instance, at regular intervals. This type of light would be marked as Al.WR (for instance, meaning alternating white and red) on a chart.

More sophisticated variations include flashing or occulting lights with the colour change superimposed on the basic rhythm. They all, however, are indicated on charts by the letters Al at the beginning of their abbreviated description, with other letters indicating the particular colours concerned.

Lights flashing Morse code characters, for instance, are often used where a particularly distinctive rhythm is required. They are particularly common around oil fields, where lights flashing the short-short-long rhythm of the Morse letter U are used to warn vessels to keep clear of exclusion zones. On charts, such lights are labelled Mo (U).

Sectored and Directional Lights

Many lighthouses and all buoys show lights that can be seen from any direction, but there are exceptions.

Lights mounted on shore or very close to the coast in particular may not be visible from some directions because they are obscured, either by the lie of the land or by nearby trees or buildings, or because they are deliberately screened to stop them annoying local residents. Where this makes the light faint or invisible from the sea, the chart may show the obscured area by dotted lines extending outward from the light.

In Figure 93, for instance, Angela Point hides the light on Misery Point from boats approaching from the east. These lines can only be approximate: a light may be perfectly visible to the watchkeeper on a ship's bridge, perhaps 20 metres above the waterline, when it would be obscured from a yacht in the same position by a sloping headland.

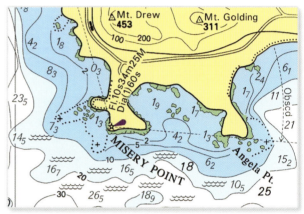

Figure 93

This principle can be put to good use in the form of sectored lights. As the name suggests, a sectored light is one that has been deliberately arranged to be visible only from certain directions, or sectors – to shine a white light down the centre of a channel, for instance, or to show a red light over a hazardous shoal. Evans Head Light Head (just right of centre in Figure 94) is a typical example. To vessels approaching it from the north-east or north-west, through either of the deep channels from Haire Sound, it shows a white light. But anyone trying the riskier approach from the north would see a red light.

In many cases, particularly where a relatively narrow channel has hazards on each side, such as in the approach to Blackmill Marina (Figure 95, page 121), it is increasingly common to find the channel itself marked by a white sector, with red and green sectors on each side so that the navigator of a vessel that strays out of the white sector can tell immediately which side of the channel he is on.

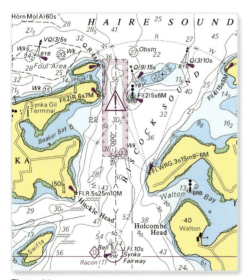

Figure 94

Of course, this information has to be shown on the relevant chart, but the sectors themselves are often omitted from smaller-scale charts of the area. The sectors of the Blackmill light, for instance, are clearly shown on the large-scale chart, but on smaller-scale coastal charts it might appear simply as Oc.WRG.6s. The fact that three colours are shown (WRG) could easily lead one to expect an alternating light rather than a sectored one. The key difference, however, is that an alternating light is always clearly identified as such, by the abbreviation 'Al'.

Directional lights are a slightly less-common variation on the same theme, in which the light is so tightly focused that it can be realistically represented on the chart by a single line.

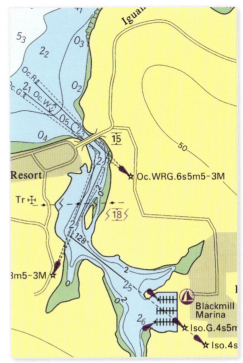

Figure 95

Buoys and Beacons

Lighthouses are vastly outnumbered by countless smaller navigation marks such as buoys and beacons, used to mark hazards and channels. These vary considerably in size: Large Automatic Navigational Buoys (Lanbys) may be up to 12 metres high and weigh as much as 140 tons, while at the other extreme some very minor channels are marked by plastic buoys not much bigger than footballs. Beacon towers are substantial brick or stone-built structures as big as some lighthouses, but the term beacon can also refer to wooden or plastic posts no bigger than telegraph poles driven into the sea bed. Perhaps the most primitive marks of all are withies, which are tree branches that have been roughly trimmed and driven into the muddy beds of creeks and rivers.

• It is a common mistake to assume that all buoys and beacons have lights: many do not.

The IALA System

Buoys and beacons are sometimes described as 'signposts of the sea'. That isn't quite true: they are more like 'Keep Left' signs, conveying information such as 'the channel is that way' or 'there is a hazard to the north of me'. Of course, it is useful if that kind of information can be instantly understood by navigators of any nationality, so the overwhelming majority of buoys and beacons nowadays conform to an international 'convention of buoyage' known as the IALA system.

There are actually two IALA systems, known as IALA B, which is used around the USA and Pacific Rim, and IALA A, which is used everywhere else. There is only one significant difference between them.

Both systems use three main groups of buoys and beacons:

- Cardinal marks are mainly used to mark hazards.
- Lateral marks are mainly used to mark the edges of well-defined channels.
- Miscellaneous marks.

Cardinal Marks

Cardinal marks are named after the four cardinal points of the compass, positioned around hazards such as sandbanks, rocks and wrecks and named to indicate the direction of the safest water. A North Cardinal is placed somewhere to the north of a hazard and has safe water to the north of it, a West Cardinal lies to the west of the hazard, and has clear water to the west, and so on. The shape of cardinal marks varies considerably, but they are all black and yellow and carry top marks consisting of two black cones. The arrangement of the colours and the shape of the cones distinguish one type from the others.

Although published diagrams often show cardinal buoys in groups of four around a hazard, this is relatively rare in practice. Very few hazards are marked on all four sides, and many have just a single cardinal buoy.

Why Two Systems?

The idea of marking hazards and channels is probably almost as old as seafaring itself, so it is hardly surprising that local areas developed their own distinctive way of doing things. Nor is it particularly surprising that things have changed: within the last hundred years Britain alone has had at least three different systems.

The Victorians handed down a system in which red conical buoys marked the starboard side of channels, with striped or chequered buoys to port. In the 1930s that was replaced by one in which the red conical buoys were replaced by black ones.

That most recent change took place gradually during the 1970s, and – amongst other things – involved changing all the black buoys to green.

It came about as part of the adoption of an international system of buoyage, devised by and named after the International Association of Lighthouse Authorities (IALA), which drew on the best features of the many different systems that were in use around the world.

One irreconcilable difference, however, was between the American and European systems. The Americans used a system similar to the one that was in use in Victorian Britain, so a red buoy meant different things on opposite sides of the Atlantic. Neither side was prepared to change to match the other.

A North Cardinal mark (Figure 96) is placed to the north of the hazard and has relatively clear water to the north of it.

Both cones point upwards and the top of its body is coloured black.

It is easy to remember if you think of the cones indicating the black part of the mark, and towards the top of the chart.

If it has a light, it will be a continuous quick or very quick: think of it as a sequence of 12 flashes to indicate that it is at twelve o'clock (i.e. straight upwards) relative to the hazard.

Figure 96

A South Cardinal mark (Figure 97) is placed to the south of the hazard, and has relatively clear water to the south of it.

Both cones point downwards, and the bottom of its body is coloured black.

Again, it is easy to remember if you think of the cones indicating the black part of the mark, and towards the bottom of the chart.

If it has a light, it will be a composite group quick or composite group very quick. The main group consists of six flashes: think of it as indicating that it is at six o'clock relative to the hazard. There is always a distinctive long flash at the end to avoid any possible confusion with the East or West Cardinals.

Figure 97

An East Cardinal mark (Figure 98) is placed to the east of the hazard, and has relatively clear water to the east of it.

Its cones point away from each other and the top and bottom of its body are coloured black with a yellow band around the middle.

Figure 98

This colour scheme too can be remembered by thinking of the cones indicating the black part of the mark. Some people find that they can remember that it is an East Cardinal by thinking of the cones as making an egg shape, or by seeing the gap between the cones as representing the Equator, or even by visualizing an E drawn around the two cones.

If it has a light, it will be a quick or very quick, flashing groups of three: think of it as being at three o'clock relative to the hazard.

A West Cardinal mark (Figure 99) is placed to the west of the hazard, and has relatively clear water to the west of it. Its cones point towards each other and the middle of its body is coloured black with yellow bands at the top and bottom.

Following the pattern set by the others, its colour scheme can be remembered by thinking of the cones indicating the black part of the mark.

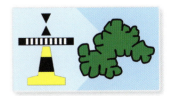

Figure 99

The top mark can be remembered either as a bobbin shape and using the mnemonic West Winds Wool, or by thinking of it as Wasp-Waisted West or by seeing it as being in the shape of a letter W turned on its side.

If it has a light, it will be a quick or very quick, flashing groups of nine, and follows the clock rule by being at 'nine o'clock' relative to the hazard.

Lateral Marks

Lateral marks are usually but not invariably used to mark the edges of reasonably well-defined channels, and are named port-hand or starboard-hand according to the side on which they are intended to be passed when you are approaching or entering harbour, or when going clockwise around a continent (the UK is not a continent! See Figure 100).

Figure 100

When leaving harbour, heading out of the river or going anticlockwise round a continent, of course, your direction of travel is reversed, but no-one comes out to switch all the buoys round for you! This means that port-hand buoys have to be left to starboard when leaving, or going anticlockwise.

The 'into harbour' and 'clockwise' rules are both straightforward enough in themselves, but there are inevitably places where they contradict each other, particularly at major headlands (such as Land's End, St David's Head and Malin Head), large estuaries (such as the Thames Estuary, Bristol Channel and the Clyde) and in the vicinity of islands.

Where there is a significant risk of ambiguity the direction of buoyage is marked on charts with a large magenta arrow symbol (as in Figure 101), and where there is an abrupt change, such as in the Solent and Menai Straits, it is shown by two such arrows, head to head.

In IALA region A, port-hand marks (Figure 101) are can-shaped or have can-shaped top marks, and are red. If a port-hand buoy has a light, it too is always red, with any rhythm that is unlikely to be confused with a preferred channel mark.

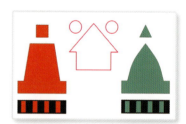

Figure 101

Starboard-hand marks are conical or have conical top marks, and are green. If a starboard-hand buoy has a light, it too is always green, with any rhythm that is unlikely to be confused with a preferred channel mark.

Where a channel forks (Figure 102), the buoy at the centre of the fork has to have a split personality, because it has to be treated as a starboard-hand buoy by vessels taking the left fork, but as a port-hand buoy for those taking the right fork.

In practice, the usual solution is to use a cardinal buoy, but the IALA convention includes preferred channel marks (Figure 103) to deal with the situation.

As can be seen they look very much like normal lateral buoys, but with the addition of a broad band of the opposite colour, and lights which flash a distinctive 2+1 rhythm. They may look complicated, but the simple rule is that if you want to follow the preferred channel, treat each one as though it were a normal lateral mark of the same shape and colour, without the band.

Figure 102

Figure 103

Miscellaneous IALA Marks

The miscellaneous group includes three completely different kinds of mark (Figure 104).

One is the safe water mark (a) positioned where there is safe water all around it. Of course, the presence of a safe water mark implies rather more than just an absence of hazard: it may mark the beginning or centreline of a channel. The buoy itself can be spherical or pillar-shaped, but it is always red and white and usually has a single red ball top mark. Its light, if it has one, is occulting, isophase, or Morse A, or sometimes a long flash every 10 seconds.

An isolated danger mark (b) also has safe water all around it, but the mark itself is positioned right on top of a hazard of relatively small size, such as a wreck or a pinnacle of rock. By their very nature, isolated danger marks are seldom found in deep water, so they are often in the form of beacon towers or beacons, rather than buoys.

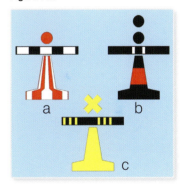

Figure 104

The distinctive features are their red and black colour, and their two black balls for a top mark. When lit, isolated danger marks show two white flashes.

Special marks (c) are the most widely used but generally the least significant of the IALA marks. They can be used to mark areas set aside for military exercises, survey work, dumping grounds, cables and pipelines, recommended anchorages, recreational areas (such as waterski areas) and as yacht racing marks.

A special mark is always yellow and if it has a topmark it is in the form of a saltire (multiplication sign). The light, too, is always yellow, if it has one, but the buoy or mark itself can be any shape. If it is can shaped or conical, though, it is best to treat it as though it were a port- or starboard-hand buoy respectively.

IALA Region B

The only difference between the buoyage conventions in IALA Region A and Region B is that in Region B the colours associated with port and starboard sides are reversed.

The shapes, however, stay the same, so an American port-hand buoy is a green can, while the corresponding starboard hand mark is a red conical – usually called a 'Nun' in the USA.

There is a corresponding difference in the Region B preferred channel marks and lights: anything that is red in Region A becomes green in region B, and vice versa.

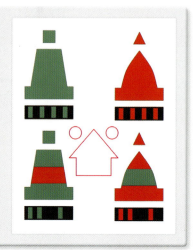

Fog Signals

Most lighthouses and some buoys and beacons are fitted with fog signals, designed to make a loud noise that can be used to identify them in fog.

Bells, gongs and whistles are used mainly on buoys, where they are operated either by the movement of the buoy itself or by machinery. Horns, usually electrically operated like giant-sized car horns but sometimes using compressed gas, are more widely used on lighthouses.

Horns and mechanically operated bells, gongs and whistles can be given distinctive characteristics, just like lights, in which case the relevant details are shown on the chart. It is important to be aware, though, that the way sound travels through waterlogged air is unpredictable: sometimes foghorns sound closer than they really are, more often they are muffled, and often their apparent direction is distorted.

Summary

Lights
- The distance at which a lighthouse can be seen depends on the brightness of the light, the height of the lighthouse and the observer, and prevailing weather conditions.
- Lights can be distinguished from one another by their characteristics: rhythm, period and colour.
- Lights can be hidden from certain directions (obscured) or they can be deliberately contrived to be visible only from certain directions (directional or sectored).

Buoys and Beacons
- Cardinal marks are generally used to mark hazards.
- Lateral marks are generally used to mark the sides of well-defined channels.
- Miscellaneous marks are used to mark the centre lines of major channels, the beginning of harbour fairways, isolated dangers surrounded by navigable water and for other special purposes.

PILOTAGE

At the beginning and end of every passage, the priorities change. The big issue isn't whether you can find your way from A to B, but whether you can get out of A and into B without hitting anything. Here, where the water is shallower and the hazards are closer, conventional navigation techniques of working out courses to steer and taking and plotting fixes are too slow and cumbersome. The situation calls for another group of techniques – collectively known as pilotage.

Pilotage need not be particularly complicated. Finding your way in and out of many artificial harbours such as Brighton or Torquay involves little more than aiming at the gap between two very solid, and very visible, pier heads.

Barely one step up in complexity is the situation found in some rivers, where the edges of the deep water channel are lined with boats on moorings. Following the channel is just a matter of following the line of clear water between the rows of moorings.

Buoy Hopping

Even in these situations it is unusual for lines of moorings to reach right out to the river mouth. More often they stop short of the entrance and the mooring buoys or piles are replaced by more widely spaced navigation marks.

Following a channel by steering from buoy to buoy is still a perfectly valid and very popular pilotage technique, but it does have a few possible pitfalls that can be overcome by taking simple precautions.

The first of these is the straightforward risk of missing a buoy or two, and thereby cutting the corner.

Approaching Rozelle Cove (Figure 105), for instance, the Fairway Buoy (at the bottom of the chart extract, just left of centre) is an obvious waypoint.

From there, the route to the Marina passes close to a starboard-hand post (green, with a triangular topmark) then dog-legs north-eastward before

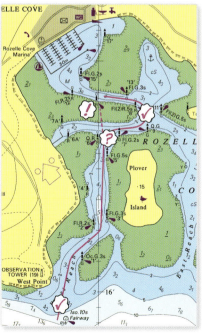

Figure 105

turning northwards again to pass between three more starboard-hand posts and their port-hand counterparts (red with cylindrical topmarks).

After passing the third of the red posts, there is another red post almost directly ahead and only a quarter of a mile away – but heading straight for it would take us right over the rocky ledge that the posts are supposed to mark.

Looking at the chart shows that the safe channel turns almost ninety degrees to starboard at this point.

The first line of defence against this trap is preparation. Make a note, either on a notepad or on the chart itself, of the bearing and distance from each mark or turning point to the next. Armed with that information, you should know exactly where to look for each buoy even before you arrive at the one before it. If the worst comes to the worst you can always turn the boat onto the required bearing and be confident that the mark you are looking for will be somewhere ahead.

Figure 106

A related problem is to lose track of which buoy you have reached, and either not to realise how far you've come or to skip a few, and believe yourself to be further on than you really are. This is particularly true of long, winding channels, where there may be literally dozens of buoys or beacons.

The defence against this one is to keep a careful record of each mark as you pass it, either ticking it off on your pre-prepared list, or by ticking it off on the chart, or by marking up each one as a single point fix (see page 62).

The most subtle trap for buoy-hoppers is caused by wind and tide.

Namley is a good example. Figure 107 is a reduced chart extract, covering an area about three miles wide, showing large areas of drying marshes, mud and sandbanks. As the tide rises, a vast quantity of water has to flow in through the relatively narrow channels between the drying areas – and of course it has to flow back out again as the tide falls. But so long as the tide is high enough to have covered the sandbanks off Warren Point (on the right-hand side of the entrance) the tidal streams don't have to follow the channels.

Figure 107

In Figure 108, a yacht has come in through the entrance, past the tide gauge beacon and the conical green buoy N3, and (at 'A') has turned almost 90° to starboard to head for the green buoy N7, close to the northern tip of Warren Point.

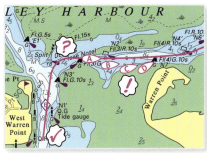

Figure 108

The outgoing tide, however, is flowing southwards, pushing her strongly sideways. At B, her helmsman is still steering straight towards the buoy, but she is well off track.

With the tide still pushing him sideways, the actual ground track achieved by simply aiming at the buoy will be a curve, bulging downtide of the intended track, and possibly coming to an abrupt halt at C or D.

Even if that doesn't happen, it can be very disorientating to arrive at a buoy from the wrong direction.

In this case, for instance, the navigator is likely to expect to see the red buoy N4 about 30° off the port bow as he approaches N7. In fact, if he's approaching from the direction of D, it will be slightly to starboard.

The best way to stop either of these things from happening is to look beyond the target mark to find some kind of landmark. It need not be on the chart: it could be a boat on a mooring, or a bush or parked car. It must, however, be stationary and likely to remain so for as long as you need it. A cow that is lying down would be OK, but one which is standing up would not!

The landmark and the target together form an impromptu transit (see page 80) which you can't easily plot on a chart, but which nevertheless provides an easy way of following a dead straight track from where you are to the buoy or beacon.

Transits (see also page 80)

The fact that an impromptu transit can be used as a way of following a straight ground track between two buoys or beacons begs the questions, "Why bother with the buoys at all: why not just follow the transit?"

This is the principle behind leading lines. A leading line consists simply of a pair of distinctive marks positioned so that they appear to be in line with each other when seen from a vessel that is following the channel.

Assuming the marks are set up on shore, so that a boat heading into the harbour is steering towards them, the secret of staying on the line is to follow the front mark. In other words if the mark nearest to you appears to be sliding to the left of the more distant mark, steer to port, and vice versa. Coming out of harbour, with the marks astern, the opposite applies: you follow the rear mark by steering to port if it drifts off to the left of the nearer mark.

Transits and Leading Lines

As with almost all navigation aids, transits and leading lines should not, as a rule, be used without referring to the chart. The mere existence of buoys, beacons or a leading line does not give any information about the depth of water, while the significance of some local marks – such as painted rocks – may not be obvious to the stranger. In the Channel Islands, for instance, some transits are called 'striking marks' because if you follow the transit you will hit a rock. Locals know that they can avoid the hazard by making sure that they keep the transit 'open'.

Figure 109

When you are not quite on a transit line, so the marks are not quite lined up with each other, the transit is described as open: you might, for instance, say the island is open to the left of the headland (Figure 109). This is nowhere near as precise as a true transit, but it can still be a useful nugget of information.

Head Marks and Back Bearings

A leading line is really just a position line that has been set up to follow the line of a harbour approach channel. Any other kind of position line would do just as well, so long as it is accurate enough.

One of the most convenient is a compass bearing, because the only requirement (apart from a reasonably accurate compass) is a suitable landmark directly in line with the intended track (Figure 110). The secret of using such a head mark or back bearing is not to try taking a bearing of the object and then try working out how to correct it. It is far better to line up the compass with the intended bearing and to look across it. If a head mark (a landmark ahead of you) is to the right of your line of sight it is almost intuitive to alter course to starboard.

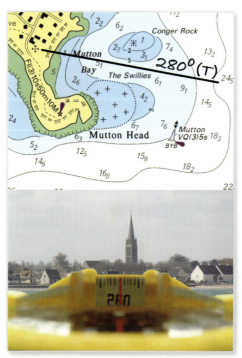

Figure 110

In many cases, especially where the tidal stream is not too strong, or is setting roughly in line with the intended track, there is no need to use a hand-bearing compass at all. It can be done by settling the boat onto that particular heading for a few seconds and checking that the head mark is, indeed, directly ahead.

The principle of a back bearing is exactly the same, except that it uses a landmark astern. This has the advantage that you will probably have passed quite close to the landmark, so it will have been easy to pick out and positively identify it, but the layout of most boats means that you will definitely have to use a hand-bearing compass to check the actual bearing. The treatment for a bearing that is not what it should be is different too: if the landmark is to the right of your line of sight across the compass you will need to alter course to port.

Turning Bearings or Wheel-Over Bearings

The essence of pilotage is that you are sticking to a pre-planned track, so it is obviously useful to know when to turn from one heading to another. Often this will be obvious, but occasionally it may not be. The easy solution is to look for a suitable landmark and say, "We'll turn when the buoy (or whatever it is) is directly abeam" (Figure 111). Unfortunately, whilst this may seem very accurate, it can magnify any existing cross-track error. As the diagram (Figure 112) shows, it is much better to use a bearing of an object that will be almost directly ahead or astern once the boat is on her new course. The next head mark is ideal.

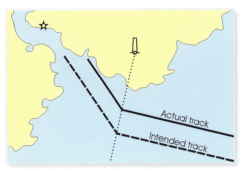

Figure 111

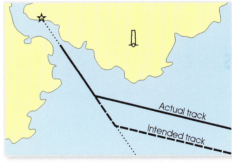

Figure 112

Clearing Lines

For some purposes, leading lines, heading marks and back bearings all suffer the same rather surprising drawback: they are just too precise!

It's impossible for a sailing boat to beat to windward up a transit line. If two motor boats meet head-on when they are both following the same leading line there is likely to be an understandable reluctance by either of the two skippers to stray far away from the line, even though there may be plenty of water on each side of it.

The solution is a powerful pilotage technique known as clearing lines. A typical example is in Figure 113, in which the approach to an anchorage lies close to some unmarked rocks.

Imagine, for a moment, that we had just touched the rocks on the eastern side of the entrance. We can see from the chart that, at the moment we touched, the bearing of the Old Light House must have been greater than 190°. If it had been 190°, we would have missed them. The line of bearing 190°, drawn through the church, is called a clearing line because it just clears the hazard.

Of course, if there were hazards on both sides of the approach we could use a second clearing line.

In this example, so long as the bearing of the church is somewhere between 270° and 290° (Figure 114), we must be somewhere in the funnel-shaped corridor of clear water in the middle of the bay.

In reality, one would probably want to allow a margin for error, but even if we were to keep the bearing of the church between 275° and 285° it would still give us a lot more room to manoeuvre than using the church as a head mark.

Of course, if the rocks to the north of the bay were not there we wouldn't need the associated clearing line, but would simply need to make sure that the bearing of the church was never more than 290°(T).

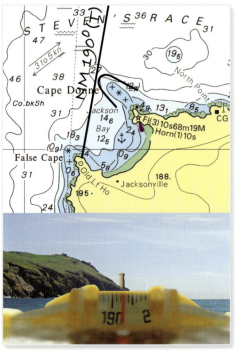

Figure 113

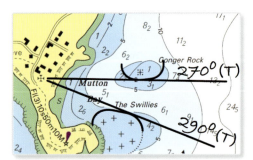

Figure 114

Sectored Lights (see also page 120)

The principle of visual clearing bearings must have been one of the influences that led to the development of sectored lights, because the similarities are obvious: the boundaries between the sectors make the edges of the safe corridor visible even without the use of a compass.

Clearing Contours

The visual clearing lines shown in Figure 113 are nothing more than position lines, drawn in advance. Any other kind of position line can be used. One of the most intuitive is an echo sounder clearing line, or clearing contour, in which the navigator states 'I don't want to go into water less than 5m deep' (or 2m, or 20m, or whatever).

Most skippers probably develop their idea of what constitutes too shallow depending on the size and type of boat, the weather conditions and sea state, and whether the local geography is hard or soft.

Using clearing contours effectively means rather more than never going into shallow water. It means picking a contour that is shallow enough to allow you to get to where you want to go, but deep enough to give adequate warning before you hit a hazard.

It is important, too, to keep an eye on the shape of the contour. If it wriggles and zig-zags too much it may be difficult to be sure which way to turn when the echo sounder says you've reached it. For all these reasons, clearing contours are seldom very useful in rocky areas. They are, however, at their best in rivers, where zig-zagging between contours that lie roughly parallel to the banks may be almost all the navigation you need.

Clearing Ranges

Ranges, particularly those measured by radar, make effective clearing lines even though they can be difficult to draw on a chart.

The principle is shown in Figure 115, showing the funnel-shaped approach to Port Fraser. The deep-water channel runs north-westwards from the bottom right-hand corner of the chart extract towards the harbour entrance (top centre). For vessels approaching from the west, the way in is partly blocked by a long sand bank, extending more than a mile offshore, but there's a useful short cut, called the 'Swashway'.

We can see from the chart that the only hazard more than 0.6 miles from the shore is Southcott Bank, and that the closest part of Southcott Bank is 0.75 miles from the coast. In other words, so long as the coast is no less than 0.6 miles away from us, but no more than 0.75 miles away, we must be in safe water.

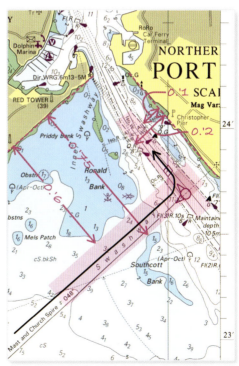

Figure 115

We could use the same technique to tell us when to turn, because we can see that the red buoys marking the port side of the channel are 0.2 miles from the eastern shoreline. So when we are within 0.2 miles of the eastern shore it is time to turn hard to port, towards the harbour entrance.

North-up Radar

The increasing availability of north-up radar, in which the radar picture is rotated to put north at the top regardless of which direction the boat is pointing, has opened the way for small-craft navigators to use one of the most powerful techniques available for 'blind pilotage' – pilotage without visible landmarks. It is called parallel indexing.

The principle of parallel indexing is that if you know the track you are intending to follow it is possible to predict the way a fixed landmark – known as the reference target – will appear to move on the radar screen.

Figure 116 shows a very simple example in which the intended track is from west to east, passing exactly a mile south of a fort. If we are to pass a mile south of it, then on the radar it should appear to pass a mile north of us, and as our track is from west to east its apparent movement should be from east to west.

Some radar sets include facilities for drawing lines electronically on their screens. Alternatively, it is possible to use a grease pencil or dry-wipe marker pen to draw either on the glass of the screen itself or on a protective acetate sheet placed in front of it.

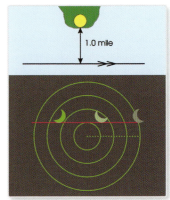

Figure 116

If, when the time comes to put the plan into practice, the contact representing the fort does, indeed, move across the screen according to plan, then we must be on track. If it does not – if it slips closer to the centre than it is supposed to, for instance – then clearly something is going wrong and we need to take steps to correct it by altering course away from the fort in order to get it back onto its planned line.

More complicated examples can be put together in much the same way, but exactly the same results can be achieved by thinking in terms of waypoints – by asking yourself "What will be the range and bearing of the reference target from each waypoint in turn?" When the results are plotted onto the radar screen, the resulting line should look very much like the intended track on the chart, scaled to suit the radar and rotated through 180° (Figure 117).

Although this is an incredibly powerful pilotage tool, it cannot be stressed too much that parallel indexing requires great care in the preparation and planning stage and skill and concentration when it comes to putting it into practice. Check and double check everything, and in particular be aware of the fact that it all depends on the reference target being visible and identifiable throughout.

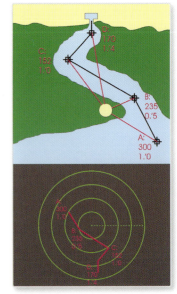

Figure 117

Electronic Pilotage

Until May 2000 the idea of using electronic position-fixing systems as anything more than a back-up system in pilotage waters was generally frowned on – and with good reason. GPS was certainly the most popular and arguably the most accurate navigation system that was readily available to civilians, but it simply wasn't accurate enough to be relied upon for much more than finding the first buoy in an approach channel.

When Selective Availability was switched off (see page 65), that changed. Few people would use GPS to follow a narrow river in broad daylight and good visibility, but there are certainly occasions on which e-pilotage is a viable proposition, and a growing number of navigators are experimenting with new techniques for using the equipment available.

Figure 118

Chart plotters and the quick plotting techniques such as waypoint webs (Figure 118) and cross-track ladders described in Chapter 6 (pages 72–73) mean that fixing and plotting procedures are quicker than they were, so standard coastal navigation can be carried on further into what would once have been regarded as pilotage waters.

Other e-pilotage techniques are adaptations of conventional pilotage, using the bearing to waypoint display as a head mark or clearing line (Figure 119).

Figure 119

Finally, there are a growing number of techniques that are aimed at making the most of the functions and features of particular pieces of equipment. Some plotters, for instance, include a facility that allows the user to mark off 'no-go zones', and will trigger an alarm if the boat crosses the boundary into one of these cordoned-off areas.

Figure 120

Setting up a boundary area like that shown in Figure 120 (where the cross-hatched area is the no-go zone) is a back-up to traditional methods, such as the leading line, but it also lets you wander around the harbour looking for a suitable mooring or anchorage without having to monitor your position constantly.

A simpler but less-sophisticated variant of this is available on some GPS sets, which include the facility for entering avoidance waypoints that trigger an alarm if you approach too close to a designated spot.

Traffic Lights

Harbours with narrow entrances, locks or swing bridges often use traffic lights to control movements. There are many local variations, often based on the familiar red means stop, green means go principle, but the following international system is becoming common:

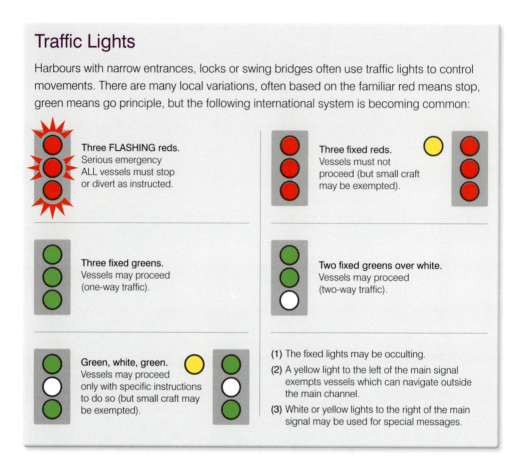

Three FLASHING reds.
Serious emergency
ALL vessels must stop
or divert as instructed.

Three fixed reds.
Vessels must not
proceed (but small craft
may be exempted).

Three fixed greens.
Vessels may proceed
(one-way traffic).

Two fixed greens over white.
Vessels may proceed
(two-way traffic).

Green, white, green.
Vessels may proceed
only with specific instructions
to do so (but small craft may
be exempted).

(1) The fixed lights may be occulting.

(2) A yellow light to the left of the main signal exempts vessels which can navigate outside the main channel.

(3) White or yellow lights to the right of the main signal may be used for special messages.

Rules and Regulations

The normal collision regulations apply in harbours and their approaches just as they do at sea, but they are often supplemented by a variety of local bye-laws and by advice from harbour authorities. This kind of advice often has much the same effect as more formal regulations, because ignoring it could be construed as an offence against some catch-all bye-law such as 'The master of a vessel in the River shall navigate the vessel with care and caution and in such a manner and at such a speed as shall not cause nuisance, annoyance, excessive wash, damage or injury nor danger of damage or injury to any other vessel, person, or property in the River nor to the banks of the River or any person or property thereon.'

Most harbour bye-laws include a speed limit (or at least an advisory speed limit). Commercial ports in particular are also likely to include some kind of regulation intended to keep small craft clear of ships by amplifying Rule 9 of the collision regulations. Harwich, for instance, has recommended routes for small craft, while Portsmouth has a compulsory small boat channel that keeps vessels under 20m tucked in to the western side of the narrow entrance.

Many harbours impose exclusion zones (Figure 121), around commercial or military wharves and jetties, or have areas such as shellfish beds where anchoring is prohibited. Southampton extends the idea of exclusion zones to cover moving ships by imposing a moving exclusion zone 1,000 metres long and 200 metres wide ahead of particularly large ships in particularly tricky parts of its approaches.

Figure 121

All commercial ports use VHF radio to control shipping movements, but few have the capacity or the inclination to handle calls from yachts. Dover is a notable exception: its regulations require small craft to obtain permission by radio before entering. Many others suggest that small craft should listen to their VHF port operations channel so as to keep in touch with likely shipping movements.

So many harbours now have local rules and regulations that researching them is an integral part of the planning stage of any pilotage. Some information (particularly on exclusion zones) is given on charts, and some is included in yachtsmen's almanacs and pilot books. Unfortunately, pilot books are usually written primarily for sailing boats, so speed limits are often omitted. Keep an eye open for notices displayed on harbour walls and beacons, or painted on buoys.

Avoid the Channel

In commercial ports it is generally best to plan your pilotage so as to stay out of the main channels. If you stay in shallow water ships can't get you and you can't obstruct them.

Planning Pilotage

Pilotage is a quick but accurate form of navigation involving minimal chartwork while under way. In order to achieve that, however, it requires considerably more planning than conventional navigation in more open water. Except in the very simplest situations it is difficult, if not impossible, to make an effective plan once you have arrived in pilotage waters. It has to be done well in advance.

For an unfamiliar port, the planning process must begin by gathering information from the largest scale chart available to you, from pilot books and almanacs, and even, perhaps, from tourist guide books and the internet, or from leaflets issued by the harbourmaster's office.

The height of tide will almost certainly be important, as may be the times of sunrise and sunset, and possibly the weather forecast.

There may be other factors that limit your freedom of movement, such as locks, swing bridges, marina cills or sand bars that can only be crossed at certain states of the tide, or mundane domestic requirements. There is no point planning a pre-dawn departure if you need to wait for a fuel barge or supermarket to open for essential supplies!

The idea at this stage is to get a general feel for the situation, whether it's a straightforward entrance between two breakwaters opening directly into a marina, or a winding channel, or whether what looks like a winding channel will turn out to be a broad expanse of open water if you arrive within a couple of hours of High Water.

The chances are that, in the process, one or more possible routes will present themselves. This is particularly true if you are using yachtsmen's pilot books, which often include 'potted' pilotage plans.

The second phase involves making a more definite plan, based on the constraints that limit your freedom to manoeuvre, the hazards that have to be avoided and the marks and techniques that could be used to avoid them. If possible, it is best to avoid relying on one technique: leading lights, for instance, become useless if one of them is temporarily obscured, but the situation can be saved if you have a compass ready to use the remaining light as a heading mark.

The plan should be marked on the chart, but many navigators also like to convert the finished plan into written notes and diagrams that can be kept in a pocket for instant reference. There is not much point reproducing the pilot book, nor in listing pages from it: the idea of the written plan – particularly in something like a RIB or in the open cockpit of a sailing boat – is to save you having to consult books and charts at every alteration of course.

To achieve this, the written plan needs to include the range and bearing of each landmark (Figure 122) from wherever you expect to be when you first see it, a description of it and what you are going to do with it – is it a head mark, a back-bearing, a clearing bearing? It should also include the direction and distance you intend to travel between each course change, and possibly a note of how critical it is for you to be on track at each stage.

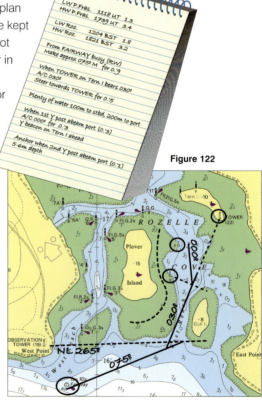

Figure 122

Pilotage in Practice

Putting pilotage into practice should, ideally, be a straightforward matter of putting the plan into practice.

To do so, it helps if the helmsman and navigator can work as a team, with the helmsman taking some responsibility for keeping the boat on track while the navigator concentrates on locating and identifying the next set of marks.

In a buoyed channel, for instance, a typical routine would involve the navigator locating the first buoy, using a hand-bearing compass and binoculars if necessary. At the right moment he would point it out to the helmsman, perhaps by referring it to some more prominent feature on the land beyond. When the helmsman has altered course, the navigator's first move must be to check that the actual course is what he expected it to be – as a double check that he has pointed out the right buoy and that the helmsman is looking at the same one – before turning his attention to the job of locating the next one.

If there is a long distance between buoys, the navigator may have to do without the luxury of picking out the next buoy quite so far in advance, but he should, in that case, take extra care to make sure that the helmsman isn't being pushed off track. This is particularly true when aiming at a single buoy with nothing beyond it to use as an impromptu transit (see page 80) or when using bearings as head marks, back bearings or clearing bearings.

Summary

- Pilotage is the art of following a planned track in confined waters, such as when entering harbour:
- Buoy hopping:
  - Following a buoyed channel by steering from one buoy to the next.
- Transits (sometimes called 'leading lines'):
  - A line defined by two objects that appear to be in line with each other.
- Head marks and back bearings:
  - A line defined by a compass bearing of a single object ahead or astern.
- Turning bearings:
  - Visual bearings used to identify the point at which to alter course.
- Clearing lines:
  - A position line that just misses a hazard: the idea is to make sure you are on the 'safe' side!
- North-up radar provides a powerful pilotage tool called parallel indexing.

11 PASSAGE MAKING

The idea of setting off into the sunset has always been part of the appeal of boating, under sail or power, but the fact of the matter is that sensible navigators – even before the SOLAS regulations made planning compulsory – have always made some form of plan if only to avoid spending too much time fighting a contrary tide, getting caught out by bad weather, or arriving after the pubs and restaurants have shut!

The legal requirement may be overkill for some passages, but for others it is very much a minimum requirement, so being able to tick off each of its six main elements (see p.141, 'The Law', section 3) does not necessarily guarantee a successful or trouble-free passage.

Planning Factors

Any journey, no matter how simple it may seem, involves several factors. The teenager on her trip to the shopping mall in Chapter 1 had a definite objective in mind (to get to a sports shop). She had certain limitations on her freedom of action, such as being dependent on her parents or buses for transport, and a number of hazards to be avoided – such as spending her bus fare on something else or getting caught in the rain. To help her, though, she probably had some local knowledge and certainly had the map at the entrance to the mall.

At sea, although the circumstances are very different, we have the same five main factors to think about:

- Objectives.
- Constraints.
- Hazards.
- Aids.
- Route.

Objectives

The objectives are the most personal of all the passage-planning features and vary enormously. The objective of the crews taking part in the Fastnet Race, for instance, is very different from that of a family setting out on a cruise to south-west Ireland, even though they are both going to much the same place!

The Law

A significant change in international law took place in July 2002, when the latest revision of the Safety of Life at Sea (SOLAS) convention came into force. For the first time in its 90-year history, the scope of SOLAS has been extended to vessels of less than 150 tons, including private pleasure craft.

Regulation 34 is one of the new rules applicable to all vessels. It says:

1. Prior to proceeding to sea, the master shall ensure that the intended voyage has been planned using the appropriate nautical charts and nautical publications for the area concerned, taking into account the guidelines and recommendations developed by the Organisation.

2. The voyage plan shall identify a route which:

* *takes into account any relevant ships' routeing systems and ensures sufficient sea room for the safe passage of the ship throughout the voyage.*
* *anticipates all known navigational hazards and adverse weather conditions; and*
* *takes into account the marine environmental protection measures that apply, and avoids, as far as possible, actions and activities which could cause damage to the environment.*

3. The owner, the charterer, or the company, as defined in regulation IX/1, operating the ship or any other person shall not prevent or restrict the master of the ship from taking or executing any decision which, in the master's professional judgement, is necessary for safe navigation and protection of the marine environment.

The International Maritime Organisation (IMO) guidelines and recommendations are geared towards larger vessels, but the UK's Maritime and Coastguard Agency (MCA) has suggested that for small craft a passage plan should include:

* *an up-to-date weather forecast • tidal predictions • the limitations of the boat and crew*
* *navigational dangers • a contingency plan • details left with a responsible person ashore*

The MCA has told the RYA that it does not expect to see a written passage plan from small craft skippers, but it is difficult to see how anyone could prove that they had made a passage plan without being able to produce it!

Constraints

One big difference between the family crew and the racing crew may well be their strength, fitness and competence. The racing crew should be able to take several days at sea in their stride while keeping the boat sailing hard throughout. A family crew, perhaps composed of a couple of 70-year-olds, with their son and daughter-in-law and a 5-year-old might well find any more than 16 hours at sea both physically and mentally exhausting. This will obviously limit the length of passage that they can undertake, though it need not prevent them from covering the same distance by breaking it up into shorter sections.

The point is that crew strength and the length and duration of the intended passage are major factors.

If you are sailing with a crew of strangers there is a lot to be said in favour of having a short 'shake down' passage on the first day of a cruise in order to assess their strengths and weaknesses.

Sunrise and Sunset

The significance of sunrise and sunset is as clear as day itself. Simply operating the boat is more demanding at night. One's ability to concentrate is reduced and everyone is more prone to cold and seasickness. For motor boats in particular, operating at night reduces the helmsman's ability to 'read the waves' to such an extent that high-speed operation can become uncomfortable or dangerous.

On the other hand, being able to see lighthouses makes night navigation in open water rather easier than by day: traditional visual fixes can be obtained at greater distances from the coast and with virtually no uncertainty about exactly what landmarks you are taking bearings of. The classic passage plan for a passage out of sight of land was always to aim to arrive off the coast at dawn, so as to take advantage of the lighthouses to get a positive fix offshore, with daylight for the pilotage on arrival.

Most yachtsmen's almanacs provide a table of sunrise and sunset times. They can also be obtained from newspapers and many GPS sets.

Tide

Many marinas have cills, intended to keep a reasonable minimum depth of water in the marina even when the tide falls outside. In such places, the rise and fall of the tide sets absolute limits on the times at which it is possible to get in or out. If you really must leave at Low Water, it can usually be arranged, but only by taking the boat out of the marina and onto a 'waiting pontoon' or mooring before the tide falls.

Similar constraints can apply to natural harbours. In some, boats are kept on drying moorings and can only leave when the tide has risen high enough for them to float. In others there may be a natural cill in the shape of a sand bar across the entrance. In the most extreme examples, such as Paimpol and Perros on the north coast of France, the falling tide may leave the harbour separated from the sea by a mile or more of damp sand and mud.

Bridges and overhead cables impose much the same restrictions, particularly on sailing yachts, except that in this case you can only pass under them when the tide is below a certain level.

Locks and Swing Bridges

Locks and swing bridges impose the same kind of constraints as marina cills, especially as their opening hours are often governed by the height of tide.

Their purpose is usually to keep as much water trapped in the basin on the shoreward side of the lock as possible, so the standard routine is for both lock gates to be opened to allow a period of 'free flow' as the tide rises.

At High Water or soon afterwards, however, the lock will be available only for one-way traffic, with a human operator opening and closing the gates to let boats in and out whilst retaining as much water as possible.

At some stage, governed either by the absence of water outside, by the design of the lock, by the need to retain water or simply by the working hours of the operator, many locks close until the next tide or the next morning.

There is invariably a pattern to their use, but it is impossible to predict without local knowledge. If you are in the port wanting to get out, the surest way to find out is to look on the harbourmaster's notice board. If you are aiming to arrive, the best advice is either to telephone ahead or to check as many sources of information, such as pilot books and almanacs, as possible. Their information on this subject is often contradictory or incomplete, but it is usually possible to find a reasonable consensus.

Tidal Streams

Tidal streams can exert a powerful influence on passage planning. Around the coasts of the UK and northern Europe their rate is often comparable with the speed of a sailing yacht or slow motor cruiser. In the case of a sailing yacht beating to windward, a fair tide can be enough to double the boat's VMG (Velocity Made Good). A foul tide, on the other hand, can bring it to a complete standstill.

For sailing boats, then, it almost always makes sense to plan a passage to make the best possible use of favourable tidal streams. This is especially true around headlands and through narrow channels, which are sometimes known as tidal gates because they can only be passed at slack water or with a fair tide.

Tidal streams can also have a significant effect on the sea state. If the wind and tide are in roughly the same direction the waves are generally longer and lower than the force of the wind might lead you to expect, with crests that are noticeably less likely to break. When the tide turns, to flow against the wind, the wave length shortens, and the waves become higher and steeper with a higher chance of breaking crests. Fast motor boats in particular may be forced to slow down in wind-against-tide conditions. For them, it may be worth making an upwind passage against the tidal stream in order to take advantage of the higher speeds that can be achieved in smoother water.

Fuel

Fuel capacity and fuel consumption impose a limit on the distance that a motor boat can cover between refuelling stops. For sailing vessels, fuel may not be quite such a critical factor in passage planning but it still has an effect: in light winds in particular your ability to make progress against the tide may depend on using an engine, or your use of lights and electronic navigation aids may be governed by the need to run the engine to recharge the batteries.

A diesel engine will stop almost instantly when air gets into its fuel system. To stop this from happening, a good rule of thumb is never to use the last 20 per cent of your tank's capacity. Petrol engines are able to tolerate an intermittent supply of fuel – such as is caused by fuel sloshing about in an almost empty tank – but their actual consumption is more difficult to predict.

Most diesel engines burn about 1 gallon of fuel per hour per 20hp (or develop about 3.3kWh per litre), so a 200hp engine can be expected to burn about 10 gallons per hour at full power, or a 10hp engine will run for about two hours on a gallon.

Petrol engines are less efficient, particularly when they are lightly loaded, but typically develop about 12–14hp.hr[15] per gallon (about 2--2.3kWh per litre).

Two strokes are the least efficient, developing about 8–10hp.hr from each gallon of fuel (1.3–1.6kWh per litre).

In theory, the power used is approximately proportional to the cube of the shaft speed (i.e. the shaft speed multiplied by itself, multiplied by itself again). This cube rule is reasonably reliable for sailing boats and slow motor boats, so it is possible to work out the likely fuel consumption:

Fuel Consumption – Planing Boats

For planing motor boats, the 'cube rule' tends to overstate the advantages of throttling back, particularly if slowing down involves running at the inefficient 'hump' speed. A better approximation can be achieved by using the formula:

$$\text{Power} = \frac{K \times \text{engine speed}^4}{\text{boat speed}}$$

e.g. A RIB has a 120hp four-stroke petrol engine, capable of 6,000rpm and 40 knots. Cruising speed is 30 knots, at 4,200rpm.

1. Find K by putting real numbers into the formula:

- $120 = \dfrac{K \times 6^4}{40}$ - $120 = \dfrac{K \times 1296}{40}$ - $K = \dfrac{120 \times 40}{1296}$

- $K = 3.7$

2. Use K to find out how much power is being developed at cruising rpm by putting real numbers into the formula:

- $\text{Power} = \dfrac{3.7 \times 4.2^4}{30}$ - $\text{Power} = \dfrac{3.7 \times 311}{30}$

- $\text{Power} = 38\text{hp}$

3. A petrol engine develops about 12–14hp.hr per gallon, so 38hp requires about 3 gallons per hour.

---

[15] Hp.hr means horsepower hour: a unit of work or energy equal to the work done by 1 horsepower in an hour.

A sailing yacht has a 10hp diesel engine, capable of 3,800 rpm, but is usually operated at about 3,000rpm.

1. At 3,800rpm, develops 10hp
2. 3,000rpm is approximately 80 per cent of maximum
3. 80 per cent x 80 per cent x 80 per cent = 51.2 per cent. So at 3,000rpm, the engine is developing about 51 per cent of 10hp = 5hp[16]
4. Diesels produce about 20hp.hr per gallon
5. This engine is producing about 5hp
6. 5hp ÷ 20hp.hr = 0.25
7. So it burns 0.25 gallon per hour at cruising rpm

Remember that:

- Calculated fuel consumption figures are less reliable than measured data.
- Fuel consumption increases in rough weather, with a fouled bottom or propeller.
- Many twin-engined boats are very slow and very inefficient when using one engine; don't assume that going slowly with one engine will give greater range.

Traffic Separation Schemes

Traffic separation schemes (TSS) have been set up in busy shipping areas in an attempt to reduce collision risks by channelling ships into clearly defined shipping lanes (Figure 123). They are shown on charts as magenta-shaded separation zones, typically a mile or two wide, or magenta-coloured separation lines, separating two or more traffic lanes that are usually up to about five miles wide. The area between a separation scheme and any adjoining coast is called an inshore traffic zone (ITZ). Traffic separation schemes are not impenetrable barriers – it is quite legitimate to enter them or cross them, but Rule 10 of the collision regulations lays down specific rules about how power-driven vessels less than 20m long and any sailing vessel should behave in the vicinity of a traffic separation scheme.

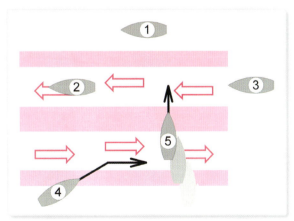

Figure 123

---

[16] Throttling back by 20 per cent reduces fuel consumption by about 50 per cent, but for non-planing boats (such as sailing boats) it may only reduce the boat's speed by a fraction of a knot.

Vessels under 20m long and sailing vessels should avoid TSS whenever possible. If you must use a TSS (see Figure 123, p.145) then:

1. Use the appropriate traffic lane and travel with the flow.

2. & 3. If possible, join and leave the TSS at its ends.

4. If you must join from one side, do so at a shallow angle, like a slip-road joining a motorway.

Avoid crossing a TSS, but if you must do so:

5. Make your course (not your track) at right angles to the traffic flow: do not allow for tidal streams or leeway.

Use your engine if necessary. Do not impede the passage of vessels using the TSS.

Course to Steer Across a TSS

The course to steer across a TSS is laid down by the rules, which say 'shall cross on a heading as nearly as practicable at right angles to the traffic flow'. This obviously affects any course-to-steer calculation.

In some respects the distance and direction you move while your course is dictated by the TSS can be treated as though it were another tidal stream vector.

1. From your intended starting point, mark off your intended track and tidal stream vectors in the usual way.

2. From the end of the tidal stream vectors, add another vector representing the course and distance required to cross the TSS.

3. Subtract the time spent crossing the TSS from the total time and estimate the distance you will travel in this time. Use this as the radius of the arc that is drawn from the end of the vectors to cut the line representing the ideal track.

4. The line drawn from the end of the vectors to the arc represents the optimum course to steer when you are NOT in the TSS.

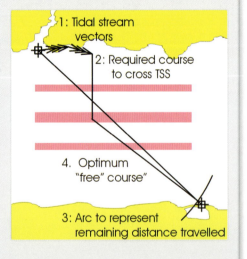

1: Tidal stream vectors

2: Required course to cross TSS

4. Optimum "free" course

3: Arc to represent remaining distance travelled

Hazards

The distinction between a constraint and a hazard is blurred, and somewhat academic: the fundamental point is that a hazard is something to be avoided. A traffic separation scheme, for instance, can be treated as a constraint (because it forces you to steer a specific course) or as a hazard (because it is likely to contain a high density of fast-moving traffic).

Rocks and Shallows

Rocks and shallow patches are obviously hazards that most navigators will usually try to avoid. Even this, though, needs some qualification: how shallow is 'shallow'? In calm water, and with a soft, muddy bottom, it may be perfectly acceptable for a sailing boat to operate with her keel barely inches above the bottom.

A motor boater, aware of his expensive and vulnerable propeller, may well want to allow a considerably bigger margin for safety, while a rocky bottom and rough water may call for an under-keel clearance (UKC) of several metres. A rock that is visible above the water, on the other hand, is so easily avoided that it ceases to be a hazard and could even become a useful landmark.

As well as the vertical margin for safety represented by the UKC, it's important to allow a horizontal margin for error in case you aren't exactly where you think you are, or in case the hazard isn't exactly where it is shown on the chart. Like the UKC, what constitutes an appropriate margin for error also varies, depending on circumstances, and it may well be acceptable to allow a smaller margin if you are dealing with a soft bottom rather than a hard one, or are in calm water rather than rough. The simple rule of thumb, though, is that you should never approach closer to a hazard than the limits of your navigational accuracy.

The increased acceptance of GPS, satellite differential and electronic chart plotters may have changed the numbers involved from miles to hundreds of metres or from hundreds of metres to tens, but it has done nothing to alter that basic principle.

Weather Hazards

The weather can change quickly and can vary quite significantly over relatively short distances, so even the best weather forecast should never be regarded as more than a rough guide. Even so, it would be stupid to ignore any available advice on a factor that can have such a profound effect on so many aspects of a passage.

Bad weather can:

* Reduce boat speed.
* Reduce the accuracy of traditional navigation.
* Reduce the reliability of electronic equipment.
* Increase fatigue.

Light winds are not usually regarded as hazards. For motor boats, the lighter the wind the better.

For sailing boats, however, very light winds rob the boat of its main motive power and may force you to fall back on the engine. On a long passage, in particular, fuel consumption then becomes a significant factor.

The main source of weather information for seafarers around the UK coast is still the shipping forecast, issued by the Meteorological Office four times a day and broadcast by the BBC on 198KHz. Twice a day it is supplemented by the Inshore Waters forecast, giving more detail of coastal waters.[17] Relevant extracts of these forecasts are also broadcast by the Coastguard on marine VHF channels.

Shipping forecasts, or similar forecasts from other sources, are often posted on harbourmasters' notice boards and at marinas and sailing clubs, and are available from the internet,[18] and from various premium-rated fax and telephone services.

Navtex is a radio telex service that produces written transcripts of weather forecasts and navigational safety information. It requires special receiving equipment, but the service itself is free, it's automatic, and its messages are in English, regardless of where in the world you happen to be.

Visibility

Poor visibility has an obvious effect on several traditional navigation techniques, because you can't take a visual bearing of something you can't see! Offshore, where you couldn't see many landmarks anyway, this doesn't make any difference, but it can be quite significant in pilotage waters, where you are more likely to be relying on visual methods.

Visibility is also a key factor in collision avoidance. There must always be a greater risk of collision in poor visibility than in good, so passage plans for poor visibility may need to be adapted to stay clear of areas where shipping traffic is likely to be heavy.

Visibility Terms

The following words are used to describe visibility in British marine weather forecasts:

Good	> 5 miles
Moderate	2–5 miles
Poor	1km–2 miles
Fog	< 1km

Fog is a more serious matter. In general, it is not advisable to set out in fog.

If you are caught out in fog, the safest tactic is to find shallow water and stay in it. If you can safely make for a harbour, do so, but beware of the risk that by doing so you may well be increasing the risk of collision with other small craft trying the same thing, or with commercial shipping whose schedules make no allowances for the weather.

---

[17] Timings have changed several times over recent years: check with yachtsmen's almanacs or with magazines such as the Radio Times.

[18] Including the Meteorological Office's own site: www.metoffice.gov.uk.

Wind and Sea State

Strong winds, as such, are seldom dangerous. It is the sea state associated with them that constitutes the hazard.

Some weather forecasts include sea-state predictions, but the terminology used relates more to the way waves look from the bridge of a substantial ship in open water than from the cockpit of a small yacht. A sea state described as 'slight', for instance, can include breaking waves over 1.25m high, whilst a moderate sea with typical wave heights of up to 2.5m may be quite capable of capsizing a small cruiser.

Nor can sea-state forecasts take account of local conditions: when the wind is blowing away from the coast, in particular, the sea may be much flatter than either the forecast sea state or the strength of the wind would lead you to expect, while the tidal stream can either flatten the sea or make it rougher than it would otherwise be.

Sea State

The following words are used to describe sea state in some British weather forecasts:

Calm – glassy	0m
Calm – rippled	0m–0.1m
Smooth	0.1m–0.5m
Slight	0.5m–1.25m
Moderate	1.25m–2.5m
Rough	2.5m–4m
Very Rough	4m–6m
High	6m–9m
Very high	9m–14m
Phenomenal	over 14m

Heights refer to the significant wave height, but any sea state may include a proportion of waves that are larger or smaller.

Overfalls

Even in otherwise calm conditions, a fast-flowing tidal stream can cause localised patches of rough water known as overfalls where it flows over an uneven sea bed. Severe overfalls can be quite enough to swamp or capsize small sailing boats, so they are best avoided. Fortunately, because they are caused by geographical factors, overfalls can be easily and accurately predicted and are often represented on charts by the distinctive wave symbol (⌇⌇⌇). Even where they are marked on the chart, however, the exact location of overfalls is likely to vary slightly as the tide changes because they are always most pronounced in the area just downtide of the object that causes them – and of course they disappear altogether when the tide is slack.

This characteristic of overfalls is important, because it means that there are two quite distinct ways of avoiding them:

- Go round them. Overfalls are usually confined to distinct areas, sometimes with a calmer passage very close inshore.
- Pass through the area at slack water.

Special Operations

Special operations include all sorts of activities such as military exercises, cable laying, dredging, surveying and various kinds of civil engineering and salvage (Figure 124). Most of these need not play a major part in passage planning. If you come across a dredger or cable layer, for instance, the normal collision regulations will deal with the situation. For the others, keep an eye open on harbourmasters' notice boards for local Notices to Mariners, and on Navtex, and listen to safety broadcasts from the Coastguard or from the vessels involved.

> **SYNKA MARINE OIL TERMINAL PROHIBITED AREAS**
>
> The areas within 450 metres of the Single Point Mooring (46°14′9N, 5°56′4W) and the Liquified Petroleum Gas Jetty (46°13′4N, 5°56′0W) are reserved for vessels berthing there. Unauthorised navigation in these areas is prohibited.
>
> **PRECAUTIONARY AREA**
>
> All vessels over 150 metres in length navigating in the Precautionary Area will be given a MOVING PROHIBITED ZONE of 1000 metres ahead and 100 metres to either side. Vessels under 20 metres in length will be prohibited from entering this ZONE.

Figure 124

Aids

Aids include all the things that are going to help you to achieve your objective, including landmarks, sea marks and distinctive contours, as well as GPS and all the techniques dealt with in this book.

Navigating at the speeds achieved by typical sailing boats or by most family motor cruisers doesn't call for much detailed preparation to be done in respect of aids, though it might be worth marking the visible ranges of important lighthouses and highlighting any sectored lights if you are likely to be seeing them at night. If you are planning to use the spider's web technique (see page 72), now is the time to mark up the chart for that too.

For high speed or short-handed navigation, or if you are operating without a proper chart table, it may also be a good idea to highlight important landmarks and features on the chart.

Route

The object of this preparatory research is not to generate pages and pages of notes! The idea is to come up with a route that achieves the objective whilst avoiding the hazards and fitting in with the constraints, and includes at least enough aids to make it a practical proposition.

Bolt Holes

At the back of one's mind too there should be the thought that things don't necessarily go according to plan, so there should be contingency plans built into your thinking, including bolt holes that can be used to shorten the trip if it is going particularly slowly, or if bad weather threatens, or if you find yourself dealing with a medical emergency or a mechanical failure.

Be optimistic as well and prepare for the possibility that things might go better than expected. What are the consequences of being ahead of schedule? Could it, for instance, be worth anchoring if you arrive at a tide gate too early or reach your destination before there is enough water to get over a bar? And if so, is there anywhere to do it?

At the very least it is worth looking at what the pilot book has to say about potential bolt holes, seeing which ones you have charts of and which ones have particular limitations such as only being accessible by day or with a certain rise of tide.

Planning on Paper

Traditional sailing yacht navigation doesn't involve drawing a route onto the chart as such: it involves setting off in the right general direction, monitoring progress by a series of fixes or EPs en route, and then adapting the course to steer as the passage unfolds.

Many navigators regarded it as unlucky to write 'From' and 'To' in the boat's log book: it was always 'From' and 'Towards'. They were equally reluctant to draw planned tracks onto the chart.

Times and practices have changed – not least because using GPS purely as a surrogate sextant or hand-bearing compass to take intermittent fixes is rather a waste of its capabilities.

By the end of the research phase of passage planning you are likely to have a pretty good idea of the route you need to take, so there is no reason not to put it on the chart, especially as by doing so you open the door to the waypoint facilities that are available from any GPS set.

Route planning, however, should not be seen as a matter of 'joining the dots' between waypoints. It should be concerned with where the route goes; the route must dictate the position of the waypoints, not vice versa.

The first step, then, is to lay a straight edge on the chart to represent the intended track from your departure point to somewhere in the vicinity of the first deliberate change of direction – probably off a headland. The chances are that the exact point at which you make the turn won't matter very much, in which case it makes sense to position the waypoint somewhere where it can easily be checked by eye (Figure 125).

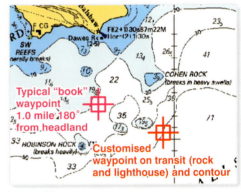

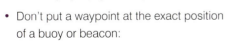

Figure 125

- Don't put a waypoint at the exact position of a buoy or beacon:

a) You might hit it.

b) There may be other vessels converging on the same point.

From that waypoint, do the same for the next leg of the route – looking backwards and forwards along both legs to make sure that neither of the intended tracks pass uncomfortably close to any hazards. Do resist the temptation, though, to take a 'battleship sweep' around headlands. It is too easy in the planning stage to put waypoints much further out to sea than they need be, either to save having to put in an additional waypoint around a headland, or to avoid the bother of having to think about whether a patch of overfalls will really be a problem at the time you are expecting to reach them. Remember that by moving your pencil an inch on the chart you may well be planning to move the boat an extra couple of miles!

Having marked up the intended track, it is certainly worth adding a note of any critical timings such as tidal gates and overfalls, and bars, locks or bridges. Depending on how you are planning to navigate the passage, it may also be worth marking in the ranges of visible lights and drawing spiders' webs (see page 72) or railway tracks (see page 73) to key waypoints. It is almost invariably worth labelling the pages of the tidal stream atlas with the clock times to which they relate, working out the times of High and Low Water at your ports of departure and arrival and measuring the distance and bearing between each waypoint and the next.

Assuming that you're going to be using an electronic position fixer, you'll need to give each waypoint a name or number and measure its latitude and longitude before entering it into the GPS. It's at this stage or during the actual keying-in that most mistakes occur. The risks can be minimised if two people share the task, with one reading out the latitude and longitude while the other keys them into the GPS. They can then be checked very quickly and easily by making sure that the ranges and bearings between waypoints indicated by the GPS are the same as those measured on the chart.

Planning on Screen

Almost all plotters include the same kind of facilities for creating and storing waypoints as are found in position fixers. They have an important advantage, though, in that you don't have to enter waypoint positions in terms of their latitudes and longitudes. In most cases there is a very much simpler procedure for creating waypoints[19] graphically (Figure 126) – in effect by just pointing at the chart image and telling the plotter where you want to go. Creating routes is usually almost as easy: just a matter of pointing at a succession of waypoints in turn.

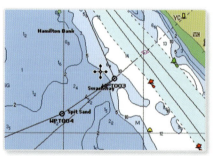

Figure 126

A slightly more sophisticated approach involves a facility often known as 'rubber banding' (Figure 127), by which you can add a waypoint between two existing waypoints and then move it, stretching the route like a rubber band to avoid obstacles. This allows you to take a broad-brush approach to passage planning, perhaps starting off with a straight line route from your departure waypoint to your destination, then adding extra waypoints to stretch your route around major headlands, before

Figure 127

[19] Some plotters distinguish between waypoints and routepoints. In such cases, the term 'waypoint' refers to a single position created in isolation, while 'routepoint' refers to one of several positions created and stored as part of the process of setting up a route.

zooming in to look at each leg of the trip in more detail (Figure 128), and perhaps adding more intermediate waypoints to deal with minor hazards that didn't show up on the small-scale, large-area picture.

The principles of positioning waypoints, however, are exactly the same whether you do it on screen or on paper:

Figure 128

- Let the route dictate the waypoints, not vice versa.
- If possible, put waypoints in positions that can be easily checked by eye when you arrive, but avoid putting them right on top of buoys or beacons.
- Do: Check the whole length of each leg of the route after you have placed the waypoint.
- Don't: Aim to pass closer to a hazard than the limits of your navigational accuracy.
- Don't: Let the scale of the chart tempt you into going miles offshore when you don't need to.

Tactical Planning

In military terms, the difference between strategy and tactics is that strategy relates to long-term plans on a fairly broad scale, while tactics relate to more short-term planning aimed at achieving a specific local objective. In navigational terms, then, the passage plan could be seen as the strategic outline. At some stage, however, the broad-brush strategic thinking of passage planning has to give way to a more tactical approach, particularly when you are faced with opposition from either the wind or tide.

	Route Report					
WAYPOINT	LATITUDE LONGITUDE	BRG M	LDST Nm	TDST Nm	TIME	FUEL
WPT001	50° 47.398N 001° 06.670W					
WPT003	50° 46.710N 001° 06.181W	159°	0.755	0.755	000:04	0.75
WPT004	50° 46.524N 001° 06.524W	233°	0.285	1.040	000:06	1.04
WPT005	50° 46.189N 001° 08.035W	254°	1.013	2.053	000:12	2.05
WPT006	50° 46.190N 001° 18.849W	274°	6.839	8.892	000:53	8.89
WPT007	50° 44.125N 001° 29.216W	256°	6.876	15.77	001:34	15.7
WPT002	50° 44.300N 001° 30.434W	287°	0.790	16.56	001:39	16.5

Figure 129

Tide Tactics

The tide always seems stronger when you are sailing against it than when it is in your favour. This is not the onset of paranoia but a mathematical fact, easily proved if you think of two boats sailing between two harbours 6 miles apart. They are both making 4 knots, but in opposite directions, and there is a 2-knot tidal stream. The tide helps one boat, increasing its speed to 6 knots, enabling it to complete the passage in an hour, thereby saving half an hour. It slows the other boat to 2 knots, increasing its passage time to 3 hours – costing it an hour and a half.

If both boats had been motor cruisers, operating at 25 knots instead of 4, the difference would have been only 2 minutes.

The moral of the story is that for slow boats the tidal stream is a force to be reckoned with, and that whilst it may be worth seeking out the strongest tide when it is in your favour it is almost always worth looking for the weakest tide when it is against you.

For faster boats the effect is less pronounced, and it may be worth fighting a stronger tide in order to stay in a stronger wind or to reduce the actual distance covered.

Wind Tactics

Wind tactics would be relatively simple if only boats really sailed upwind at 45° to the true wind and tacked through 90°. In reality, though, the wind that propels a sailing boat is much the same as the wind felt by her crew and by her wind instruments: it is the apparent wind, created from a combination of the true wind – which is what they would feel if the boat were anchored – and an induced wind created by the boat's own movement through the air that surrounds her.

Figure 130

Imagine, for a moment, a boat at a mooring on a perfectly windless day, So long as she stays attached to the mooring, her anemometer reads zero because there is no wind. Now suppose she drops the mooring and motors forward at 5 knots (Figure 130). Because she is now moving through the air, her crew and instruments will feel a 5-knot breeze, apparently coming from dead ahead, that has been induced by her forward movement.

Now suppose she encounters a 3-knot tidal stream pushing her sideways (Figure 131). She is no longer moving forwards through the air, but crabbing at an angle of about 40°, so the induced wind is about 40° off the bow. She's also moving rather faster than 5 knots through the air, so the breeze appears to freshen slightly.

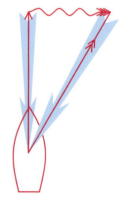

Figure 131

Now suppose a real 5-knot breeze pipes up, blowing directly across her heading (Figure 132). No-one on board can feel it, nor can it be detected by her instruments. What they perceive is the combined effect of all three factors – boat movement, tidal stream and true wind. In this particular case they joined forces rather nicely to produce a pleasant 9-knot breeze, just forward of the beam.

The apparent wind depends on six factors:

- Boat heading.
- Boat speed.
- Tidal stream set.
- Tidal stream rate.
- Wind strength.
- Wind direction.

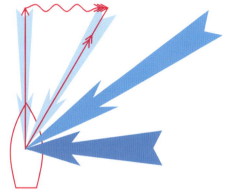

Figure 132

Wind tactics involve picking your course – the only one over which you have direct control – so as to get the best combination of all six.

Whole books could be (and have been) written about this subject alone but, rather than juggling with half a dozen inter-related variables, many navigators prefer to use a few relatively simple rules of thumb.

Lee-Bowing the Tide

The reason the apparent wind in Figure 132 was so much stronger than the true wind was because the tidal stream was pushing the boat towards the wind. If the tide had been well forward of the beam it would also have moved the apparent wind aft, making it possible to sail closer to the true wind. In other words, by putting the tidal stream on the boat's lee bow the boat benefits two ways: from a 'freeing' wind shift and from an increase in the wind strength.

The lee bow effect is most pronounced in light winds and strong tides, especially if the wind and tide are at roughly right angles to each other, and can be used to particularly good effect if the tide is due to turn during the course of a long beat to windward. It needs to be applied with caution, though, if the wind is expected to shift.

Steer Towards the Shift

If the wind and tide could be relied upon to remain constant throughout a passage it would make no difference whether you started a beat to windward on port tack (with the wind blowing over the port side) or starboard, or even whether you used a couple of long tacks or a very much larger number of short ones. The wind, however, is rarely that consistent.

The idea of steering towards the shift is very simple. In Figure 133, the skipper of the white boat knows that the wind is forecast to veer (to shift clockwise) from north-north-west to north-north-east. At some stage in the future, then, it will be impossible to steer north-north-east, because it will be directly to windward. At the start of the passage, however, he can easily steer north-north-east – so he does so. Every mile sailed close-hauled with the old wind is equivalent to a mile gained directly to windward, or about 1.5 miles sailed with the forecast wind.

The rule can be summed up as 'choose the tack that allows you to steer as close to the forecast wind as possible, or if the wind is due to shift to the right, set off on port tack.' Anyone with a background in dinghy racing may recognise that the effect is much the same as 'tack on a header'.

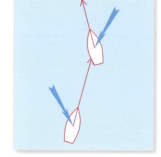

Figure 133

Close the Coast on Port Tack

A follow up to the 'steer towards the shift' rule stems from the fact that the wind on land is always some 20°–30° to the left of the wind at sea. A northerly breeze over the land, for instance, is likely to turn into something more like a north-easterly at sea.

In other words, a boat approaching a coastline can expect the wind to back progressively within 5 miles or so of the coast. To conform to the 'steer towards the shifts' rule, the aim should be to be on starboard tack at first, ready to tack when the coastal effect becomes noticeable, so as to make the final approach with a freeing wind on port tack (Figure 134).

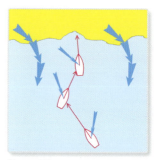

Figure 134

Cone and Corridor Tactics

Not all wind shifts are predictable and, whilst it is nice to benefit from an unexpected 'freeing' wind shift (one that turns a beat into a close reach), it is so desperately disheartening to find that a 'header' has effectively set you back to where you were a couple of hours before that many navigators adopt a policy of damage limitation known as the cone, or a variation of it that could be called the cone and corridor.

The basic idea is that by staying within a funnel-shaped approach sector directly downwind of the next waypoint you can never be badly caught out.

Drawing the cone onto the chart is easy: start by drawing the downwind line from the waypoint, then add two more lines at angles of about twenty degrees to the downwind line and both passing through the same waypoint (Figure 135).

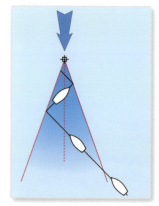

Figure 135

Exactly how wide or how long the cone should be is a matter of individual judgement and preference; the wider the cone, the greater the risk of being caught out, but the fewer the tacks you will have to make to stay inside it. Its centreline need not even lie directly downwind of the waypoint. Racing navigators often choose to skew the cone to one side or the other because they think a wind shift one way is more likely, or because one side of the line has more wind or a more favourable tide.

The similarities to clearing bearings (see page 133) are obvious; the edges of the cones are straight lines of bearing, radiating outwards from the waypoint. This makes GPS a particularly useful tool for staying within the cone. In Figure 135, for instance, the edges of the cone are 340° and 020°, so staying within the cone is a simple matter of tacking whenever the bearing to waypoint display reads 340° or 020°.

One problem with the cone tactic is that on a long passage the first few tacks may be very long, while the crew is fresh and keen to be doing something. Several hours later, when they are more tired and less enthusiastic, the tacks come thick and fast.

An alternative is to adapt the cone into a parallel-sided corridor. Again, the starting point is to draw a downwind line, then add parallel lines equally spaced on each side of it. The distance between the lines, like the width of the cone, is a matter of individual judgement, but for a family cruiser in open water it could well be in the order of 2–4 miles (Figure 136).

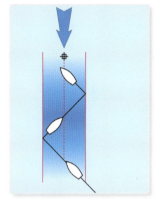

Figure 136

Like the cone, the corridor lends itself particularly well to electronic navigation, though it is slightly more complicated to set up. The principle is that the GPS needs to be told that the intended track is represented by the downwind line, rather than the line from the previous waypoint. It can then be set to sound an alarm whenever the cross-track error reaches the limit represented by the edges of the corridor.

How you achieve this in practice varies from one set to another. It may, for instance, involve temporarily abandoning the route navigation mode (in which the GPS set automatically switches its attention from one waypoint to the next) and selecting the windward waypoint as a 'Go To Target', starting at the moment you cross the downwind line.

Lay Lines

Perhaps the most important of all upwind tactics involves what are known as lay lines (Figure 137) – lines representing the ground track of the boat if she is just capable of reaching the waypoint or the windward mark without tacking. On the assumption that you don't want to spend any more time beating to windward than necessary, you should aim never to cross a lay line without immediately tacking to sail along it.

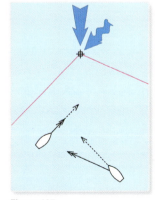

Figure 137

On the assumption that the wind and tidal stream are reasonably constant, i.e. that you are thinking about the lay line when you are already fairly close to the waypoint, it is very easy to find the direction of the lay lines by noting the track shown by the GPS while sailing close-hauled on each tack.

They don't even have to be drawn on the chart: so long as you know the direction of each lay line you will know when you reach the lay line by looking at the bearing to waypoint display.

If, for some reason, you can't use this method – if you are not using GPS, or if the wind or tide are likely to change between when you are working out the lay lines and when you will need to use them, or if the tidal stream will be very different in your approach to the buoy than the one you are currently experiencing, then you may need to resort to more traditional methods. There are several ways of doing it, including pure arithmetic and a variety of chart-plotting techniques, but by far the simplest is to guess where the lay lines are likely to be and estimate what your course is likely to be on each tack, and then to work out a predicted EP (see page 110) from an arbitrary starting point somewhere on each of the guessed lay lines.

Figure 138

The predicted EPs will give you predicted ground tracks, which can then be used to refine your original guessed lay lines, as in Figure 138.[20]

Passage-Making Routine

On passage, in any boat, the navigator's principal task is to monitor the boat's position and progress and compare it with the plan. If everything is going according to plan, obviously there is no pressing need to do anything in particular.

It's if things are not going according to plan that you will need to do something about it. The first move, in that case, must be to make sure that the boat is in no immediate danger – that a bigger-than-expected cross-track error, for instance, does not mean that she is about to go aground. The second is to decide whether to adapt the original plan to take account of the changed circumstances or to attempt to recover the original plan.

In very general terms, sailing boats and slow motor boats are very much at the mercy of winds and tidal streams over which the navigator has no control, but have the luxury of time and of a relatively stable (albeit possibly tilted) chart table in which to adapt the plan. Planing motor boats usually have more control over their speed and direction of movement, but changing the plan is more difficult, so it is generally better to try to recover the original plan.

Monitoring position and movement is not a continuous process and there is certainly no need for the navigator to keep his nose glued to the chart or plotter. A good navigator or skipper/navigator is certainly likely to make frequent checks of the course being steered, of the depth of water and of any visible landmarks. From time to time, however, a slightly more formal approach is called for.

---

[20] For the sake of clarity, the wind in Figure 138 has been assumed to be the same on both sides of the waypoint. In practice, it is likely that the apparent wind in the stronger tide will be different in both strength and direction from that in the weaker tide.

Waypoint Arrival

Most electronic navigators include a waypoint arrival alarm. As well as alerting the helmsman or navigator to the fact that the boat has reached a waypoint, this often serves to switch the system's attention to the next waypoint in a route and may be used to signal a course alteration to an autopilot.

An interfaced GPS/autopilot system should never be set up to make major alterations of course without human intervention.

In most cases, the waypoint arrival alarm is triggered solely by proximity: when your position is within a certain distance of the waypoint the alarm will sound. The distance can be set to suit the circumstances, but in general it should never be less than the accuracy of the system (currently about 0.01 miles for GPS). In most cases it is better to use a considerably bigger alarm radius so that you don't commit yourself to having to hit every waypoint accurately in order to use the automatic route-following facility.

It is seldom necessary or desirable to set the arrival radius to less than about 0.05 miles or more than about 0.25 miles.

Some systems offer a variety of more sophisticated options, such as triggering when the waypoint is abeam or when you pass a line that bisects the angle between the present leg of the route and the next.

Whatever type of waypoint arrival alarm you use, it is important to be aware of its implications. Altering course just because the waypoint alarm has sounded is a bad idea!

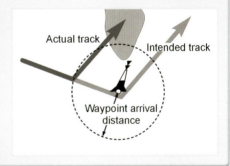

The most obvious of these special occasions is as you approach a waypoint or make some other significant alteration of course. Shortly before reaching the waypoint, the navigator will need to check the intended track and calculate the course to steer to achieve it. At or near the waypoint, he should check that it is the right one or that he is in the right place – helmsmen have been known to steer for the wrong buoy! At this stage it is also useful to record the position, time and the new course to steer.

As you leave the waypoint, check that the boat is settled on the correct course and estimate the time to go or time of arrival at the next waypoint.

- Don't rely exclusively on the chart and compass. If there are visible landmarks, make sure that what is meant to be in front of you really is in front, rather than behind or off to one side.

If the waypoints are only a matter of minutes apart, there is little need for anything else. On longer legs it is important to make similar, intermediate checks at regular intervals. On a Channel crossing of 60 or a hundred miles, for instance, one would probably carry out a routine check (or delegate someone else to do it) once an hour.

Record Keeping

Ships are legally obliged to keep a formal record of navigational events, known as a deck log. Although this requirement does not extend to private pleasure craft, it is still useful to keep some kind of record of what has happened. If someone knocks the GPS aerial off or the batteries go flat, it is very much easier to work out where you are if you have a record of where you were half an hour ago than if you vaguely remember that you passed such and such buoy 'just after tea time'. Even if such things don't happen, the deck log can be an interesting souvenir and will gradually build up into a long-term record of how your boat performs in different conditions.

The Conventional Deck Log

The deck log does not have to be an imposing, gold-embossed book: any notebook will do, though a hard-backed type is preferable. Each page should be headed with the date and a summary of the day's objectives, (such as From and To). Many owners like to include a list of who was on board. The deck log is also a good place to note the important details of your passage plan, especially the weather forecast, and tide times and heights of tide.

The main part of each page, however, should be ruled off into columns, so that each line can show the time, the course, and the log reading. Other columns can be added. Motor boaters, for instance, may want to include the oil pressure and engine temperature readings, while sailors may include wind speed and direction, but the most useful one will be a very wide column headed remarks – which will include your position. The general idea is that there should be enough information available in the deck log for you to be able to work up a reasonably accurate EP (see page 110) at any stage of the trip.

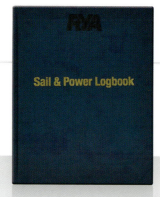

The RYA Sail & Power Logbook (G109) can be purchased at **www.rya.org.uk/shop**.

Flight Plan

A variation on the traditional deck log is sometimes known as a flight plan, because the idea comes from the very detailed flight plans prepared by air navigators. It is particularly useful for fast motor boats, because although it looks very much like a conventional deck log, the key point is that as much of it as possible is filled in in advance. The waypoints, for instance, are listed in order, but the time of passing each one is left out until it has been passed. The intended track and distance to go are filled in at the planning stage, in their own separate columns, but the course and speed (or log) columns are left blank.

Log on Chart

Another increasingly popular alternative is to use the chart itself as a kind of logbook. In fact, although this was once regarded as 'bad practice', it is really no more than a logical extension of the 'best practice' of labelling every fix or EP with the time to which it relates, and is in keeping with the Royal Navy practice of labelling course lines with the course and speed.

The one requirement, if log-on-chart is to work successfully, is to be as neat and methodical as possible. Use standard chartwork symbols for different types of position and types of line, and stick to them.

Tape Recordings

Dictating machines or small tape recorders are sometimes favoured by navigators on very small or very fast boats, on which more conventional record keeping is impossible. As a last line of defence they are better than nothing, but they are less reliable than pencil and paper, and referring back to a particular entry is difficult.

Most chart plotters and some GPS sets include an automatic logging facility. Whilst this may be interesting, and may help you learn more about your boat's behaviour or performance, a computerised record in the memory of a chart plotter is not much use if an electrical failure means that you are trying to reconstruct your position on a paper chart, and the data recorded is often minimal: most versions record time and position, many include track and ground speed. Very few record the course you are trying to steer, the tidal stream, estimated leeway or the log reading.

Lost and Found

There are many different ways of getting lost, though the experience is becoming much less common than it once was. They can, however, be divided into two fundamentally different categories.

One is when you are quite convinced that you know where you are, but are wrong. This is the kind of 'lost' that is most likely to lead to serious accidents. It happens when you bend your perception of your surroundings to convince yourself that what you can see is what you expected to see – by saying to yourself (for instance) that "that thing that looks like a factory chimney can't really be a chimney: it must be the lighthouse I was looking for. And of course I wouldn't expect to see the radio masts at this distance."

The other is the dawning realisation that something is not quite right. It happens when the tall thing on the skyline turns out to be a chimney instead of a lighthouse, or when the buoy that you were expecting to see doesn't show up.

The first job, when you realise that you don't know where you are, is to make sure that things aren't going to get worse. This may mean altering course parallel to the coast or even away from it, or slowing down, or coming to a complete standstill by turning head to tide.

The next step is to reconstruct an EP from the information contained in the deck log. This may reveal the problem, such as a wrongly plotted course or a tidal stream atlas that has been marked up from the wrong month's tide tables.

If it doesn't, resolving the situation is likely to call for more skill and ingenuity than not getting lost in the first place, because you will have to embark on some navigational detective work to think what might have gone wrong – have you, for instance, been making more leeway than you thought? Or less? It is likely to involve a lot of trial and error too, as you plot fixes based on any landmark you can see in order to find two or three position lines that produce a reasonable fix that tallies with the depth of water and your best-guess EP.

Landfall

A third, much happier kind of 'lost' is when you make a landfall – the exciting first sight of land after a passage in open water. Electronic navigation has robbed the moment of some of its magic; one waypoint is, after all, very much the same as any other, but there is still the interesting transition to be made from offshore and coastal navigation to pilotage.

For the navigator who chooses to rely on traditional methods or who has been forced to switch to them, there is inevitably an air of uncertainty about a landfall that has a lot in common with being lost. You do, however, have a number of important factors on your side. The first of these is that you have no reason to disbelieve your EP. It may not be very accurate (see pools of errors on page 113) but at least you don't know that it is wrong! The second is that you have some degree of choice over where to get lost. You may, for instance, choose to aim straight for a particularly conspicuous feature such as a large lighthouse in the expectation of being able to see it even if your EP is a few miles out.

If you are aiming for a coastline that is made up of fairly small but deeply indented bays, the best strategy is usually to aim for the middle of a bay, expecting to see at least one of the headlands on each side of it before you really need a more precise position.

Perhaps the most difficult situation is posed by a flat and featureless coastline. In this case, the only reliable strategy is deliberately to aim off to one side of your intended destination – usually the uptide side. The logic behind this is that if you aim straight for your objective but don't see it when you arrive, you have no idea which way to turn. If, however, you have deliberately aimed for a point somewhere to the east of your target, then there is a fair bet that you will find it by turning to the west, and can use the contours as clearing lines (see pages 131–132) until you can achieve a positive position fix.

Summary

- An effective passage plan is likely to involve:
  - An objective.
  - Constraints – things that limit your freedom of action.
  - Hazards – things that need to be avoided.
  - Aids – things that will help you.
  - Bolt holes in case you need to shorten the passage or seek shelter or repairs.
- The route should dictate where you put your waypoints (not vice versa!):
  - Don't put waypoints at the exact position of buoys or beacons.
  - Do check the whole length of each leg of the route.
  - Don't aim to pass closer to a hazard than the accuracy of your navigation.
  - Don't let the scale of the chart tempt you into going further offshore than you need around headlands.
- On passage:
  - Monitor position and progress.
  - Keep a record of navigational events.
  - Be ready to adapt the plan if necessary.

INTERFACING

Marine instruments always used to be separate entities, each getting on with its own job of measuring speed, or depth, etc. They can work much more effectively, though, if they can share information. This is particularly true of the more sophisticated instruments such as radars and plotters. An autopilot, for instance, needs heading information from a compass if it is to work at all, but can work even better if it also has cross-track error information from a position fixer.

Until the early 1980s, different manufacturers achieved this communication in different ways. You couldn't link a pilot from one with a position fixer from someone else, so each customer was effectively locked-in to one supplier. To solve the problem, the National Marine Electronics Association (of America) devised a standard interface – a common language that would allow one manufacturer's products to communicate with another's.

In the early 1980s there were several different versions of the NMEA code, but pretty well all marine instruments produced between 1990 and 2010 are capable of communicating with each other through an interface known as NMEA 0183.

Many more recent instruments also use a newer interface called NMEA 2000, but NMEA 0183 is still the most widespread standard.

NMEA Basics

The NMEA interfaces were originally intended for one-way communication between two instruments. In NMEA jargon they are called the 'talker' and the 'listener'. Nowadays, though, it's quite common to find one talker sending information to several listeners – a single GPS, for instance, might send information to an autopilot, a plotter, a radar and a DSC radio.

The talker produces data in the form of a string of short, low-voltage electrical pulses, which are transmitted to each listener through a pair of wires (or through two cores of a multi-cored cable) (Figure 139).

Figure 139

This simple connection starts to look more complicated when you add more listeners to the system, or when a single instrument is capable of acting as a talker as well as a listener.

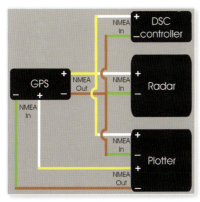

Figure 140

In order to do this it needs an outlet 'port' (pair of wires) as well as an inlet 'port' (another pair of wires) (Figure 140).

Connected to the same plug there may well be two more wires leading to the transducer or aerial, and perhaps the red and black power cables as well. To reduce the number of wires involved, it's quite common to find one negative wire serving the NMEA outlet, NMEA inlet and power supply (Figures 141 and 142).

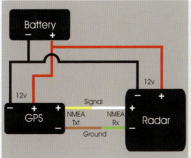

Figure 141

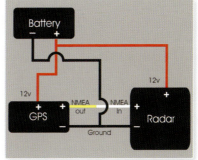

Figure 142

NMEA Code

You can visualise the pulses themselves as a sophisticated kind of Morse code, in which different sequences of pulses indicate different letters or characters. It's identical, in fact, to the ASCII code used by computers (Figure 143).

Figure 143

A series of characters make up a word, and a string of words make up a 'sentence', following strict rules of 'grammar' and 'punctuation' that are laid down as part of the NMEA specification (Figure 144).

Each sentence, for instance, has to begin with a dollar sign, immediately followed by a two-letter sequence identifying the source of the information and a three-letter abbreviation identifying the kind of information. $GPGLL, for instance, means that the rest of the sentence contains latitude and longitude from a GPS.

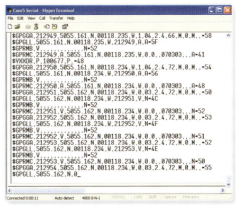

Figure 144

NMEA Problems

Although NMEA 0183 was conceived as a universal language, it wasn't without its problems. Some of these were caused by manufacturers interpreting the details of the NMEA sentence structure in different ways – a human being would probably recognise 1° 18'.58W and 001° 18'.580W as being the same, but a computer might not, so such apparently trivial details sometimes assumed enormous importance.

Problems still arise when one instrument has been programmed to listen out for one particular sentence, while another instrument is supplying the necessary information but under a different heading. The GGA sentence, for instance, might be ignored by an instrument that was looking for GLL, even though both sentences include position data.

Another common problem arose from the wide spread of voltages used by different manufacturers. Some instruments designed to operate near NMEA's upper limit (about 6 volts) simply couldn't use the pulses of one or two volts that some manufacturers preferred.

NMEA 0183 in Practice

Most of these problems have been resolved by the introduction of more refined versions of the NMEA 0183 standard. In general terms, it is now fair to say that if you have two instruments that are both claimed to use NMEA 0183, you shouldn't have any problems getting them to talk to each other. If you do have problems, then the first step is to carry out a simple four-point check:

1. Make sure the NMEA output of one is connected to the NMEA input of the other, and that the ends of any unused cores in a multi-core cable are insulated from each other and taped back.
   - Remember that one talker can communicate with several listeners, but each listener can listen to only one talker.
2. Make sure positive wires are connected to positive and negative to negative.
   - In this context, Signal, Data and Live are all synonymous with Positive, while Ground, Earth and Common are synonymous with Negative.
   - The NMEA negative wire may be connected to the battery negative, but the NMEA positive wire must never be connected directly to the battery.
3. Make sure that both instruments are set up to send or receive NMEA data. You may need to get into a set-up menu to switch the interface facility 'on' or to select NMEA instead of a proprietary interface.
4. Make sure NMEA messages are being transmitted. The easiest way is to connect a digital voltmeter between the signal and return wires. The voltmeter won't respond quickly enough to show individual pulses, but should show a fluctuating voltage of about 0.5–3.0 volts.

If, after all this, there is still a communication failure, the most likely explanation is that the listener is listening for sentences that are not being transmitted. Ideally you need to check this before you buy, because there is no simple cure for it. Unfortunately, checking before you buy isn't always easy as, although the necessary information is freely available, it is usually in the instruction manual rather than on the outside of the packaging.

NMEA 2000

NMEA 2000 – sometimes called 'N2K' – is more than just an updated version of NMEA 0183. It's a complete redesign, combining a communications protocol that has been thoroughly tried and tested in the automotive industry (CANbus) with rugged cabling and connectors that were originally designed for use in automated industrial equipment (DeviceNet).

Under the new system, power, data and control messages are carried through a single five-cored 'trunk' or 'backbone' cable. Tee connectors can be included in the backbone at any point, allowing for the connection of 'drop lines' through which any suitable instrument can receive power and can send or receive information to and from the rest of the network.

One crucial difference between NMEA 2000 and NMEA 0183 is that NMEA 2000 uses a process known as CSMA (Carrier Sensed Multiple Access) to allow up to 50 different devices to communicate with each other, rather than allowing only one 'talker' and just a handful of 'listeners'. CSMA means that before a device transmits information it listens to make sure that some other device isn't in the process of sending a message. If the network is quiet at that particular instant, it goes ahead and transmits. If the network is busy, it waits its turn.

Another key feature of NMEA 2000 is that the specification defines the shape, size and colour of the cables and connectors to be used. Using standardised plugs, sockets and cabling makes connection quick, simple and reliable, with far fewer opportunities for anyone to make a mistake or for a connection to fail. So connecting an NMEA 2000 device into an NMEA 2000 network is as simple as plugging a USB device into the USB port of your computer at home.

Another similarity between NMEA 2000 and USB is that the NMEA 2000 network cables and connectors carry power as well as data. It's not designed for high-power equipment such as radars or autopilot drives, but it's enough for most electronics.

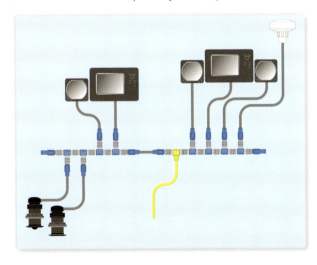

Loran is the last survivor of what was once a large and influential family of electronic position-fixing systems that include Decca, Consol and Omega, amongst others.

It was originally developed by the USA for military purposes as a LOng Range Aid to Navigation during the Second World War.

In those days, accurate clocks such as those that are fundamental to GPS were not available, but technology did allow the accurate measurement of small intervals of time.

The principle of any hyperbolic system is that if two radio transmitters transmit a signal at the same time, and a receiver receives both signals simultaneously, then the receiver must be an equal distance from the two transmitters. If one signal is received slightly earlier than the other, the receiver must be closer to whichever transmitter's signal was received first. By measuring the time difference between the two signals, it is possible to work out how much nearer, and from that, to construct a curving position line in the shape of a hyperbola (Figure 145).

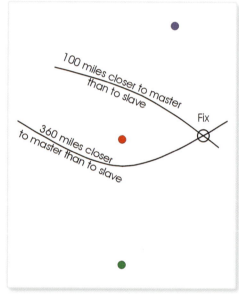

100 miles closer to master than to slave

360 miles closer to master than to slave

Fix

Figure 145

Adding a third station to the pattern means that there are two pairs of transmitters, which between them produce two position lines to give a fix.

In practice, Loran stations are grouped into chains, each consisting of several 'slave' transmitters grouped around a 'master'. They all transmit at the same frequency (100kHz), but within each chain the master transmits first, giving a distinctive signal consisting of nine short pulses lasting a total of one-hundredth of a second. The slaves then transmit in turn, giving identical signals consisting of eight pulses, at precisely timed intervals.

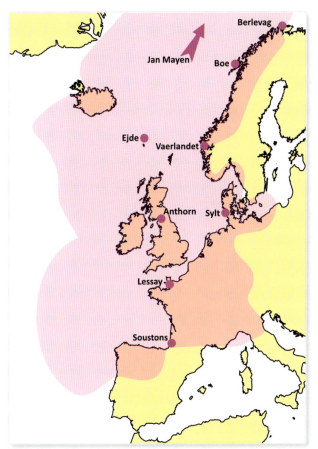

Figure 146

One chain, for instance, is based around a master station at Lessay. Soustons transmits 13.0 milliseconds (ms) after Lessay. Anthorn transmits 27.3 milliseconds after Lessay. Sylt transmits 42.1 milliseconds after Lessay.

67.31 milliseconds after it transmitted, Lessay begins the sequence all over again.

If, for instance, the Anthorn signal reaches the receiver 26ms after the Lessay signal – despite setting out 27ms later – the receiver can calculate that it has completed its journey 1 millisecond quicker. Knowing that radio waves travel at 162,000 nautical miles per second this means the receiver must be somewhere on the curving position line that is 162 nautical miles closer to Anthorn than to Lessay.

Repeating the process with the signals received from Sylt or Soustons would produce a second position line, to give a fix.

Unfortunately the speed of radio wave propagation, on which the whole system depends, is quite significantly affected by the terrain over which the signals must pass, so Loran is prone to errors that – to navigators who have become accustomed to metric levels of accuracy from GPS – seem huge.

The latest version of Loran is called eLoran. It incorporates several major improvements over earlier versions (Loran A and Loran C) and could become a viable back-up for commercial and military purposes in case satellite systems were ever blocked or jammed. But at present (2013) no-one is making or selling Loran receivers suitable for recreational craft.

Radar works just like an echo sounder. It transmits short pulses of energy and listens for the echoes produced when the pulses are reflected from something in their path.

Of course, there are significant differences between radar and an echo sounder. One is that radar sweeps its beam of pulses around the horizon like the beam of a lighthouse, instead of sending them all downwards. Another is that it uses super-high-frequency radio waves – microwaves – rather than sound waves.

Microwaves travel much faster than sound waves, so everything connected with radar happens very quickly. At its longest range setting, for instance, a typical small-boat radar produces about 1,000 pulses per second, each lasting less than a millionth of a second. At short ranges the pulses are even shorter, and there are many more of them.

The result is that every rotation of the scanner gathers information about hundreds of targets, from thousands of echoes:

- Range information from the time taken for each pulse to travel out and back.
- Bearing information from the direction the antenna was pointing when each echo was received.

It then processes data to convert it to a form that we can understand. Almost invariably, in marine radar, this is in the form of a Plan Position Indicator (PPI), in which the position of ships, buoys, boats and coastlines is shown in a map-like presentation. It's important to appreciate, though, that the PPI isn't really a map: it's a diagram showing the range and bearing of echoes.

Getting a Picture

Until a few years ago radar sets bristled with knobs and buttons. Now, knobs and buttons are 'out' and menu systems and soft keys are 'in'. Somewhere on the front panel or hidden in the menu system, though, all radars have the same main controls. Six of these are concerned with getting a picture and four with improving it. Others deal with more advanced functions, including the measurement of ranges and bearings.

1. On-Off

It's pretty obvious that if you don't switch it on, the radar won't work, but it's still a good idea to check with the instruction manual, because turning it off can sometimes be trickier!

2. Standby – Transmit

A radar doesn't burst into life as soon as you switch the power on. Most sets go through a self-test routine, like a desk-top computer, followed by a warm-up process that is intended to protect the transmitter from sudden temperature changes. There's usually an on-screen timer to show you how the warm-up process is going, but it won't transmit until you operate the transmit control.

3. Brilliance and Contrast

Brilliance is like the brightness control on a TV. It doesn't affect what is in the picture, just whether you can see it, so set it to whatever you feel most comfortable with.

Some Liquid Crystal Displays (LCDs) have one extra control, called contrast, which can turn the screen completely black or completely white. The 'right' setting is somewhere between the two, but it varies depending on your angle of view. Again, the 'right' setting is whatever you feel most comfortable with.

4. Gain

Gain is like the squelch control on a VHF radio. It regulates the radar's sensitivity. If it is too low (Figure 147), weak echoes won't appear, but if it is too high (Figure 148), the whole screen will be filled with a snowstorm of speckles. A lot of books tell you to adjust the gain 'to leave a light background speckle', which was fine for old-fashioned 'radial scan' radars. On most modern radars, though, it's best to turn it down until they just fade (Figure 149). Ignore the cluster of particularly stubborn speckles around the centre of the picture: they are a different symptom, with a different cure.

Figure 147   Figure 148   Figure 149

5. Range

It's pretty obvious that the range control changes the scale of the radar picture, but it does other things as well. In particular, at long range the radar transmits longer pulses and waits longer between pulses than at short range. The result is that you may get a slightly better picture if you use the shortest range that will do the job.

6. Tuning

We all know that a radio can only receive signals if it is tuned to match the transmitter, but it still seems odd that a radar needs to be tuned to listen for echoes of its own transmissions, unless you appreciate that the echoes are very, very weak indeed, and that the frequency produced by the magnetron (transmitter) inevitably varies slightly as it warms up and cools down.

Fine tuning is the key to a good radar picture, so although it's often automated it's worth spending a minute or so, once every few hours, to check the tuning by hand.

Purists say – quite rightly – that you should retune whenever you change range. On the other hand, because tuning is most important at long ranges, a reasonable compromise is to tune the radar on one of its longer range scales – 12 miles or more. Pick a weak contact somewhere near the edge of the screen and concentrate on that while you tweak the tuning control. Adjust it in small steps, and leave about three seconds between each tweak to allow it to take effect, until the contact is as big, bright and consistent as possible.

Improving the Picture

Those six controls are the ones that determine whether you will get a picture at all, and how good it will be. Some of them may be automated but it's still worth knowing how to adjust them manually. It's like photography: an automatic camera will take competent pictures, but a good photographer will take better ones by setting up his camera by hand.

The aim of the first set of controls is to make sure that you can see every echo the radar receives. Most of the next group are more concerned with decluttering the screen by removing the echoes we don't want.

7. Sea Clutter

The sea clutter control removes the mass of speckles around the centre of the screen caused by radar waves reflecting from the sea (Figure 150). It's not a particularly subtle control: it works by reducing the gain applied to echoes at short ranges. That makes it quite capable of wiping out real targets as well as clutter, so you mustn't overdo it (Figure 151). Treat it like hot chilli – if in doubt, leave it out!

Figure 150   **Figure 151**

8. Rain Clutter

The rain clutter control is much more subtle and innocuous. It removes clutter caused by rain and heavy cloud by ignoring everything except the leading edge of the returning echoes. This weakens the drawn-out returns from rainstorms so that they become invisible, but leaves the crisper returns from ships and cliffs unscathed. Even so, it can still weaken the echoes from some real targets, especially from gently sloping coastlines, so it's best switched off unless you really need it.

9. Interference Rejection

The IR control removes the pattern of large speckles or streaks that would otherwise appear when your radar picks up other people's transmissions. Some books and manuals accuse the IR control of deleting radar beacons from the display, but this only applies to some IR circuits and some radar beacons. It's really very rare, so you can safely leave the IR circuit switched on.

10. Echo Stretch or Expansion

Echo stretch is almost self-explanatory: it artificially lengthens each contact to make small contacts more noticeable. Unfortunately, it also makes coastlines less distinct, so although it's useful for collision avoidance it's best switched off for pilotage.

Display Mode

Until recently, it was fair to say that your own boat was always at the centre of the screen, pointing straight upwards. Because you're fixed at the centre of the screen, the rest of the world seems to move around you, so this type of display is called Relative Motion, and because you are heading straight up the screen, it's called Head-Up.

For some jobs, this is fine. It's good for collision avoidance because it's easy to relate what is on the screen to what you see around you: anything on the left-hand side of the screen is on the port side of the boat and so on. The drawback is that it can be difficult to relate the radar picture to the chart.

Most radars sold, however, can be interfaced to a compass, and can then turn their pictures round to put north at the top. This North-Up mode is good for pilotage, but also has the important advantage that it stabilises the radar picture to stop it swinging when the boat yaws.

There's nothing special about north: it's just as easy to put any other direction at the top. One particularly useful direction is your course (that's the direction you are intending to steer, as opposed to your heading, which is the direction the bows happen to be pointing!). The advantage of Course-Up is that it produces a stabilised picture but with the 'left-to-port, right-to-starboard' simplicity of head-up. One thing to be careful of when using course-up is that you must remember to switch it off and on again when you alter course, otherwise the radar will stay locked-on to your old course.

Understanding the Picture

At first sight, a radar picture seems just a mass of blobs. The general shapes of coastlines are usually easy to pick out, but some of the details, along with ships, boats and buoys, are harder to identify. To understand what the radar is seeing, we need to remind ourselves that the radar picture isn't a map: it's a diagram showing the range and bearing of echoes.

Shadows and Horizons

To produce an echo, an object must receive a radar pulse. It can't do that if there's something in the way!

Common obstructions are things like headlands or large ships, which block the radar's view of things beyond them. Radar can see in the dark or in fog, but it's no better at seeing round corners than you or I!

The biggest obstruction of all is the Earth itself. Like us, radar can see tall objects at great distances because they stand up above the horizon, and it gains a bit more because the scanner is usually higher than eye level. It gains another little bit because radar waves bend very slightly to follow the curve of the earth, but its range is still limited by a horizon.

It's easy to calculate the distance to your radar's horizon: it's about $2.2 \times \sqrt{H}$ where H is the height of the scanner in metres and the answer is in miles. So if your scanner is 4m above the water, its horizon is about four and a half miles away. If it's 9m high, its horizon is six and a half miles away. That may not sound very much but remember that a big ship may well be over 25m high, which means its superstructure will be visible when it is 10 miles beyond the horizon.

Reflections

We often talk about targets 'reflecting' radar waves, but that isn't really true. What happens is that some things absorb radar energy and re-radiate it. Others absorb them but don't re-radiate, while others don't absorb them at all, and are effectively transparent. To be a good 'reflector' or re-radiator, the target needs to be made of something that conducts electricity.

Assuming the target is made of a suitable material, four other factors decide how strong an echo it will produce.

Size is pretty obvious. A big object can reflect more energy than a small one.

Shape and orientation are important, because the energy is re-radiated at right angles to the surface. This means that a flat surface is a very good reflector, so long as it is at right angles to the approaching radar beam. If it isn't, it will bounce the echo away in the wrong direction. A curved surface is less efficient because only a small part of it can be at 90° to the beam. It's likely to be a reliable reflector, though, because if it's tilted or rotated, a different bit of the surface will be available to return an echo.

Texture is really a combination of shape and orientation: a rough surface – which in radar terms means one with lumps and bumps measured in centimetres rather than in microns – is almost certain to reflect some energy back in the right direction, whereas a smooth one will produce a better reflection, but is more likely to send it the wrong way.

Discrimination

Perhaps the biggest source of confusion, particularly on small radars, is called beamwidth effect or bearing discrimination.

Manufacturers try to produce scanners that focus the microwaves into as tight a beam as possible, but they are fighting the laws of physics. To get a narrow beam, you need a big scanner, so the narrowest you can get from an 18-inch radome is a fan shape about 5° across. Even this is only a nominal measurement: some of the energy is scattered beyond the edges of the main beam (Figure 152).

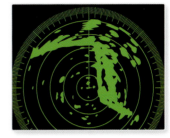

Figure 152

This means that a good reflector will produce an echo before the scanner is actually pointing at it, and go on producing an echo even after the main beam has swept past. The radar can't 'know' this: it merely detects the echo and paints it onto the screen in the direction the antenna is pointing. The end result is that small targets appear on the screen as streaks, 5°–10° degrees across, while coastlines appear smudgy, like a map drawn with a thick felt-tip pen instead of a fine ballpoint. The edges of narrow gaps, such as harbour entrances, look swollen, so the gap may disappear altogether until you get close enough for the beam to pass straight through it, and a ship may appear to block the entrance completely.

Things like this aren't 'faults' any more than not being able to sail straight into the wind is a 'fault' on a sailing boat. They are just characteristics of the system. The way to deal with them is to be aware that they happen and to get used to looking at the world with a radar's eye.

Measuring Ranges and Bearings

With only one or two very rare exceptions, even the most basic small boat radars are equipped with facilities for measuring ranges and bearings, though the details of how they are activated and operated vary from one make and model to another.

The Electronic Bearing Line (EBL) appears as a line (often dotted or broken) that extends outwards from the centre of the radar picture to its edge and which can be moved around the screen like the seconds-hand of a watch by means of one of the controls on the radar's front panel. The bearing represented by the EBL is shown in a data box, usually in one corner of the screen.

To take a bearing of a small contact such as a buoy or another vessel, position the EBL so that it cuts through the centre of the contact that represents the target. To take a bearing of something like a headland, the effect of beam width needs to be considered by positioning the EBL so that it cuts through the headland rather than brushing its tip. The offset needs to be about half the radar's beam width.

In a head-up radar, the bearing shown is always relative to the boat's heading at that particular moment. A contact on the port bow, for instance, would appear on a bearing of 315°, regardless of its compass bearing. A relative bearing can always be converted to a true bearing by adding the boat's heading, and subtracting 360° if necessary. If, for instance, we were steering 200° (Compass) at the moment a bearing was measured as 315° (Relative), the Compass bearing of that particular target would be:

315°	(Relative)
+ 200°	(Compass)
515°	
- 360°	
155°	(Compass)

It may then need to be corrected for variation and deviation in the usual way.

Beamwidth, steering errors and various other factors make radar bearings much less accurate and reliable than radar ranges.

The Variable Range Marker (VRM) appears as a circle, centred on the centre of the radar picture, whose radius can be varied by means of one of the controls on the radar's front panel. The range represented by the VRM is shown in a data box, usually in one corner of the screen.

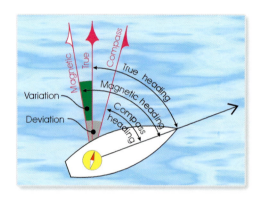

To measure the range of a target, expand the VRM so that it just brushes the closest part of the contact.

So long as the set has been properly installed and adjusted according to the manufacturer's instructions, radar range measurements are generally accurate to about 1 per cent of the range scale in use.

Cursors, like those on computers and usually in the form of a 'cross-hair' or target marker, are available on many radars. The range and bearing of the cursor from the centre of the screen are displayed in a data box, usually in one corner of the screen. Whilst it is often convenient to have a single control to measure range and bearing simultaneously, many users prefer to use the VRM and EBL.

Floating VRMs and EBLs are an increasingly common feature. They work in much the same way as conventional VRMs and EBLs, but can be positioned anywhere on the screen so they can be used to measure the range and bearing of one object from another, or as an electronic means of drawing on the screen.

APPENDIX 4

TIDE LEVELS & DATUMS

When reading a chart it is essential to remember that the actual depth of water and the heights of charted objects almost never correspond with the soundings and elevations shown on the chart. This diagram sums up the most important levels and datums involved with heights, depths and tidal calculations.

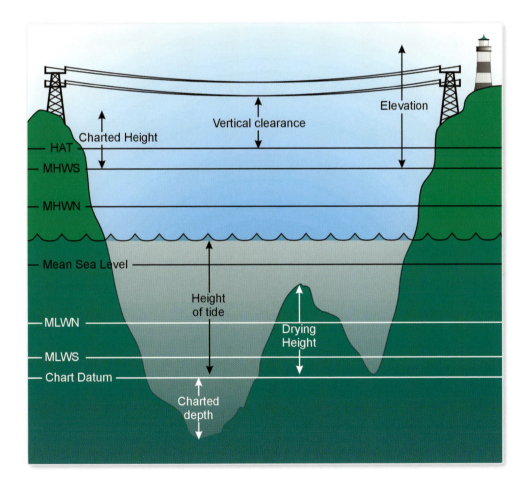

ADMIRALTY CHART SYMBOLS

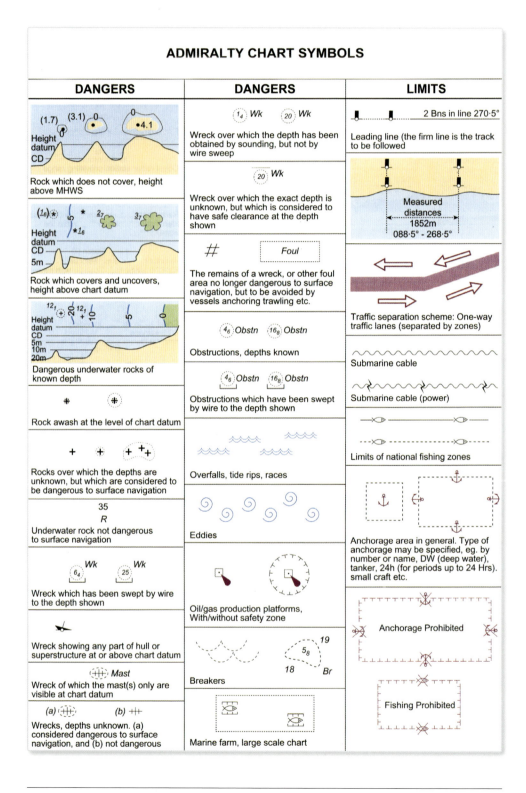

DANGERS	DANGERS	LIMITS

DANGERS

(1.7) (3.1) 0 0 •4.1

Height datum CD

Rock which does not cover, height above MHWS

(1_6) 2_7 3_7 $*1_6$

Height datum CD 5m

Rock which covers and uncovers, height above chart datum

12_1 20 12_1 10 5 0

Height datum CD 5m 10m 20m

Dangerous underwater rocks of known depth

Rock awash at the level of chart datum

Rocks over which the depths are unknown, but which are considered to be dangerous to surface navigation

35
R

Underwater rock not dangerous to surface navigation

6_4 Wk   25 Wk

Wreck which has been swept by wire to the depth shown

Wreck showing any part of hull or superstructure at or above chart datum

Mast

Wreck of which the mast(s) only are visible at chart datum

(a)   (b) +++

Wrecks, depths unknown. (a) considered dangerous to surface navigation, and (b) not dangerous

DANGERS

1_4 Wk   20 Wk

Wreck over which the depth has been obtained by sounding, but not by wire sweep

20 Wk

Wreck over which the exact depth is unknown, but which is considered to have safe clearance at the depth shown

Foul

The remains of a wreck, or other foul area no longer dangerous to surface navigation, but to be avoided by vessels anchoring trawling etc.

4_6 Obstn 16_8 Obstn

Obstructions, depths known

4_6 Obstn 16_8 Obstn

Obstructions which have been swept by wire to the depth shown

Overfalls, tide rips, races

Eddies

Oil/gas production platforms, With/without safety zone

19
5_8
18   Br

Breakers

Marine farm, large scale chart

LIMITS

2 Bns in line 270·5°

Leading line (the firm line is the track to be followed

Measured distances
1852m
088·5° - 268·5°

Traffic separation scheme: One-way traffic lanes (separated by zones)

Submarine cable

Submarine cable (power)

Limits of national fishing zones

Anchorage area in general. Type of anchorage may be specified, eg. by number or name, DW (deep water), tanker, 24h (for periods up to 24 Hrs). small craft etc.

Anchorage Prohibited

Fishing Prohibited

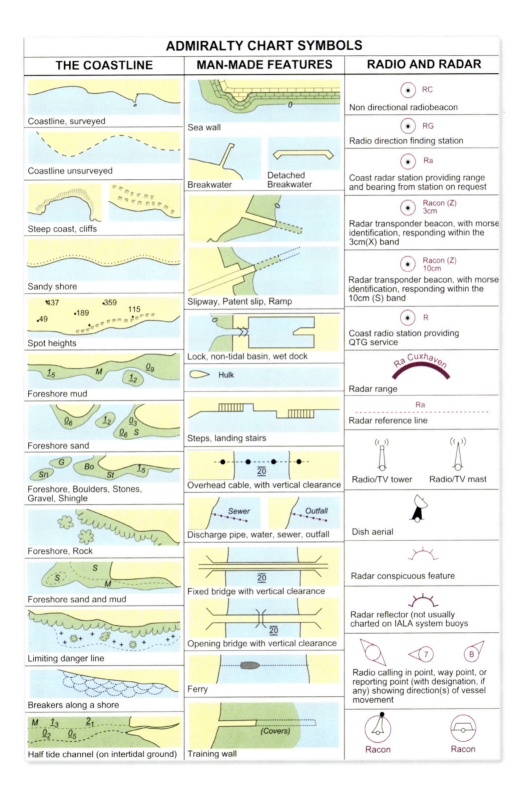

ADMIRALTY CHART SYMBOLS

THE COASTLINE	MAN-MADE FEATURES	RADIO AND RADAR
Coastline, surveyed	Sea wall	RC — Non directional radiobeacon
Coastline unsurveyed	Breakwater / Detached Breakwater	RG — Radio direction finding station
Steep coast, cliffs		Ra — Coast radar station providing range and bearing from station on request
Sandy shore	Slipway, Patent slip, Ramp	Racon (Z) 3cm — Radar transponder beacon, with morse identification, responding within the 3cm(X) band
Spot heights	Lock, non-tidal basin, wet dock	Racon (Z) 10cm — Radar transponder beacon, with morse identification, responding within the 10cm (S) band
Foreshore mud	Hulk	R — Coast radio station providing QTG service
Foreshore sand	Steps, landing stairs	Radar range
Foreshore, Boulders, Stones, Gravel, Shingle	Overhead cable, with vertical clearance	Ra — Radar reference line
Foreshore, Rock	Discharge pipe, water, sewer, outfall	Radio/TV tower / Radio/TV mast
Foreshore sand and mud	Fixed bridge with vertical clearance	Dish aerial
Limiting danger line	Opening bridge with vertical clearance	Radar conspicuous feature
Breakers along a shore	Ferry	Radar reflector (not usually charted on IALA system buoys
Half tide channel (on intertidal ground)	Training wall (Covers)	Radio calling in point, way point, or reporting point (with designation, if any) showing direction(s) of vessel movement / Racon / Racon

GLOSSARY

ARCS	Admiralty Raster Chart System
Back bearings	Taking a bearing on a landmark astern to determine position
Barycentre	Combined centre of mass of the Earth and Moon
Bearing	Direction of one object from another
Beidou	Chinese GPS system
Buoy hopping	Following a buoyed channel by steering from one buoy to the next
CadET rule	Used in calculating compass variation error
Candelas	Units of power of lighthouses
Cardinal marks	Buoys positioned around hazards, named after points of compass, to indicate direction of safest water
Cardinal points	The four main points of the compass (North, South, East and West)
Chart Datum	Level of water from which charted depths/heights displayed on chart are measured
Chart plotter	Electronic charting system; *see also* Plotter
Clearing contours	Pilotage technique where specific depths are followed
Clearing lines	Position line to clear hazards
CMG	Course Made Good; *see also* Track Angle
Cocked hat	Three position lines drawn on chart from different bearings to establish vessel's position
CoG	Course over Ground; *see also* Track Angle
Compass roses	Representations of compass card on chart
Contour lines	Lines on maps/charts linking points of equal height/depth
Course	Direction the vessel is intended to be steered
Datums	Fixed starting-points of horizontal and vertical graticules
Dead Reckoning	Position based on distance and direction travelled through water from known position
Deviation	Compass error caused by presence of magnetic objects
dGPS	Differential Global Positioning System: GPS monitoring stations
Dipping distance	Distance at which lighthouse disappears below horizon at night
Directional light	Light focused in one direction
Drying height	Height of anything above the 0-metre contour (drying line) uncovered by receding tide
ECDIS	Electronic Chart Display and Information System
Echo sounder	Electronic depth measuring device
ED 50	European Datum 1950 standard

EGNOS	European Geostationary Navigational Overlay System: GPS development
ENC	Electronic Navigational Chart
ETRS 89	European Terrestrial Reference System 1989 datum standard
Fix	Establishing position on chart
Flight plan	Variation on traditional deck log
Flux gate	Type of magnetic compass
Galileo	European GPS system
Geoid	Mean Sea Level
Glonass	Global Navigation Satellite System: Russian GPS system
GNSS	Global Navigational Satellite System
GPS	Global Positioning System: Satellite-based navigation tool
Graticules	Network of lines on chart representing meridians and parallels
Greenwich meridian	Theoretical vertical line running around the Earth from North Pole to South Pole through Greenwich Observatory
Ground track	see Track Angle
HAT	Highest Astronomical Tide: Highest level to which tide is ever expected to rise
Head mark	Landmark ahead of the vessel
Heading	Direction in which vessel is actually pointing at any given moment
IALA	International Association of Lighthouse Authorities
IALA Region A	Buoyage and beacon system used worldwide apart from USA and Pacific Rim
IALA Region B	Buoyage and beacon system used in USA and Pacific Rim
Interpolation	Calculations of tide heights at a given time
Isophase light	Flashing light with equal intervals of light and dark
Knot	One nautical mile per hour
Lateral marks	Buoys marking edges of well-defined channels
Latitude	Distance from the Equator, expressed as an angle, measured in degrees at the centre of the Earth
Lay lines	Lines representing ground track of vessel if just capable of reaching waypoint or windward mark without tacking
Leading lines	Pair of distinctive marks positioned so as to appear in line with each other when seen from vessel following channel
Leeway	Sideways movement of vessel moving through water, caused by wind
Log	Device for measuring speed through water
Longitude	Distance from the prime meridian, expressed as an angle, measured in degrees at the centre of the Earth

Meridians	Theoretical vertical lines running around the Earth at every ten degrees of longitude
MHWS	Mean High Water Springs: Average level reached by High Water over succession of spring tides
Nautical mile	1,852 metres: Average length of a sea mile
Neap tides	Lower tides brought about when tides caused by the Sun and Moon work against each other
Notices to Mariners	Weekly publications of chart amendments by UKHO
Occulting light	Intermittent light where periods of light are longer
One in Sixty Rule	Used in calculation of course to steer taking into account tidal stream
OSGB 36	Ordnance Survey Great Britain 1936 datum standard
Overfalls	Patches of rough water where tidal streams flow over uneven sea bed
Parallel indexing	Pilotage without visible landmarks using north-up radar
Parallels of latitude	Theoretical horizontal lines running around the Earth at every ten degrees of latitude
Plotter	Navigation instrument consisting of protractor, grid and ruler
Prime meridian	Theoretical vertical line running around the Earth from North Pole to South Pole through Greenwich Observatory
Railway line plot	Parallel lines drawn on chart to deal with cross-track error
Raster chart	Direct electronic copy or scan of existing paper chart
RCDS	Raster Chart Display System
Rhumb line	Line drawn on Mercator chart crossing all meridians of longitude at same angle
Rising distance	Distance at which lighthouse appears above horizon at night
RNC	Raster Navigational Chart
Rule of Twelfths	Mathematical process for estimating height of tide at given time between High and Low Water
sdGPS	Satellite differential GPS: Development of GPS
Sea mile	One minute of arc measured along meridian at earth's surface
Sectored light	Light arranged to be visible only from certain directions
SOLAS	Safety Of Life At Sea convention
Spheroids	Symmetrical mathematical models of the Earth
Spider's web	Compass rose and concentric range rings drawn around a point on a chart
Spot depth	Depth below chart datum of a particular point on the sea bed
Spring tides	Higher tides brought about when tides caused by the Sun and Moon coincide
Standard ports	Ports where tides are monitored and recorded

Tidal diamonds	Symbols on charts indicating tidal streams
Tidal streams	Horizontal movements of tides
Track Angle	Direction the vessel is actually moving over surface of the Earth
Transits	Taking bearings by lining up two static objects/features
TSS	Traffic Separation Scheme
Turning bearings	Visual bearings used to identify point at which to alter course
UKC	Under-Keel Clearance
UKHO	United Kingdom Hydrographic Office
Variation	Discrepancy between Magnetic North and True North
Vector chart	Chart format showing series of points and lines that make up features
WAAS	American Wide Area Augmentation System GPS development
Wake Course	Direction vessel is moving through the water
Water Track	Direction vessel is moving through the water
Waypoints	GPS position-storing facility
WGS 84	World Geodetic System 1984 datum standard
XTE	Cross-track error: Distance strayed from route on GPS

INDEX

M

N

O

P